The Hearts of Men

By Michael Vernon Harding

ISBN# 9798876766168

The Hearts of Men
Written by
Michael Vernon Harding

Editing by
David and Lisa Webster

Publishing Assistance
Sue Breeding
P.O. Box 1785
Columbus, IN 4722

"… He is sifting out the hearts of men before his judgment seat…"

The Battle Hymn of the Republic

Remembering
Kenny,
Deni,
and the Lunchbox Gold

Prologue

As with the first day of all New Year's past, it began with optimism and high expectations. The previous evening's celebrations had taken place at an unprecedented level, and prospects for the coming century appeared exceptional. On January 1, 2000, a new Millennium dawned. The twenty-first century had finally come, and Americans were turning the corner on one hundred years of wars and overseas conflicts. However, in the next few years of universally perceived prosperity, war was brought to the shores of the United States on the wings of its own technology and against the architectural symbols of its success. Perhaps it was the fall of the World Trade Center Towers that contributed to what happened next.

Disasters create perceived opportunity. The flames of wildfires may destroy tall, mature trees, but each large plant that is lost is replaced by literally thousands of smaller species like grasses, weeds, and other colonizers. When stressed, many animals seek to reproduce more of their kind to improve the chances of species survival. Fueled by government programs that encouraged banks to make loans based on stated income and loose credit, residential building was unrestrained in the first decade of the new millennium, and literally everyone, regardless of age or economic status, was presented with the opportunity to achieve the American Dream: to own their own home.

Families of modest income saw a chance to quit paying rent and buy property for the first time in their lives; young college graduates seized the opportunity to achieve in a short time frame what their parents had acquired through decades of hard work; insecure thirty and forty-somethings unwilling to gamble on an uncertain future took out second and third mortgages on their homes; and speculators purchased real estate opportunity with no money down, counting on the bounce from flipping their Ponzi properties before the whole system collapsed, which of course, it inevitably did.

In some parts of the country like Las Vegas, Phoenix, and Southern California, home lots were sold numerous times – for a profit – before the streets were even rough-graded and before a single foundation was poured. The pace of building was frenetic as well as the hiring of men and women to plan, construct, and sell the domino developments of urban sprawl. Everyone seemed to be making money off the boom: bankers, middlemen-lenders, builders, real estate brokers, carpenters, plumbers, electricians, landscapers, irrigation specialists, and especially local and state governments who salivated at the thought of future income from property taxes and, more importantly, budgeted and spent the money before it materialized.

It is often said that the pilot of a doomed airplane will continue to fly his aircraft right up to the moment of impact. When the housing bubble burst, it was as sudden and the fall as steep as the Dow Jones Industrial Average on Wall Street. There seemed to be no bottom to it, and the sinkhole sucked in everyone even remotely connected to the building industry. When the hammers fell silent, land clearing stopped too, and the big yellow machines were parked; barren earth bled into storm drains and streams; vertical forests of bright-framed walls and floor joists faded in the summer sun and twisted in the winter snow.

As in the great decade of the Dust Bowl, the country became a financial wasteland as the economy took a downturn. Hard working people of every stripe lost their jobs – from professionals to plumbers. In an ever-tightening spiral of helplessness, many people despaired. Families were shattered by divorce as the epidemic of unrelenting unemployment destroyed the will of the wage earner. Still other families consolidated, pooling shelter and economic resources for the long, slow recovery. The rate of suicide increased, and more people showed up in hospital emergency rooms. Newspapers reported the occasional story of a mother and father taking their lives – and sometimes those of their children – shamed by failure. Loan defaults and foreclosures reached unimaginable levels even as the government bailed out banks whose loan policies had created the problem in the first place.

Housing prices dropped precipitously; mortgage interest rates were at an all-time low; a good time to buy perhaps, but the banks were holding their bailout money close to their chests and making no loans. In despair, people whose home values had dropped as much as twenty-five to fifty percent simply quit paying their mortgages. Government programs that were intended to help struggling owners keep their homes were a morass of bureaucracy and bank intransigence. They only served to extend the insecurity and despair of those that had any hope left at all. Like a summer shower that falls from high clouds as virga but never reaches the parched land, the unkept, politicized promise of redemption is pitiless.

When a bull enters the ring, there is little doubt concerning the outcome. The animal wrongly assumes that if it puts up a fight it will survive. It exerts enormous effort, playing the game because it has no choice. The bull repeatedly charges the proffered, beautiful, and enticing cape, gasping for air after each thrust, mucus stringing from its mouth and nostrils, sweat running uncontrollably down its flanks. In contrast, the matador gracefully pirouettes and arches his back, preening his superiority. The bull is weakened as its life's blood is released by the actions of the picador. With colorful bandoliers sprouting from his shoulders like party favors, he is barely able to stand when the matador ends his life with a quick, thin sword–thrust between the shoulder blades. Through the matador, the banker, and the mortgage broker, such cruelty reveals the hearts of men.

1

The city bus squealed to a protracted stop at the street corner, just as it and others like it had done countless times every day over many years of service to this inner-city community. An exhalation of pressurized air escaped from somewhere under the bus as the side doors opened and a young man stepped out into the bright sunshine. From inside the cool darkness of the interior, a man handed down an olive-drab duffle bag.

"Thanks for your service," the stranger said to the soldier.

Another sound: this time of air pressure building up in pneumatic hoses as the bus doors flapped shut and air brakes were released. With an electric hum the bus eased away from the curb, hot dust kicking away from the exhaust panels in its side. The young man closed his eyes and held his breath for a moment as the fugitive particles and diesel fumes vortexed around him. Slinging the strap of the cylindrical canvas bag over his shoulder, he started down the street.

His uniform was the mottled tan and brown camouflage fatigue that had been designed specifically for desert warfare; his boots were the color of sand. Although the duffle contained everything that he owned, he shouldered it without effort; he was bronzed and fit from many tours of duty in the Middle East.

The first thing Donovan Owens noticed was the lack of traffic and people on the street. Over the years of his absence, he had nurtured a physical memory of his old neighborhood: the hum of lawnmowers, the smell of fresh-cut grass mixed with smoke from backyard barbecues, the shuffle and cry of young boys playing soccer in the street and silent girls sitting on front steps watching them, mothers and grandmothers watching the girls from the cool shade of a porch swing.

He had visualized a Hollywood homecoming: pausing to kick a soccer ball with the kids in the street while still shouldering his duffle, rubbing a few of the boys' heads as the young girls on the steps at first hesitated, then running into the house to announce his unexpected return. His mother would appear at the top of the steps wiping her hands on her apron, for she would be in the process of preparing supper. From the back yard, he would hear the lawnmower stop abruptly as if it had been stalled by tall grass. There would be his father in the driveway, walking quickly but dignified toward him, grasping him by the shoulders, looking him straight and severely in the eyes before breaking into a broad smile. As people large and small gathered around him, the old man would drape his big right arm over his son's shoulders and extend his left hand like an opera singer, announcing to the neighborhood: "Our boy is home!"

What Don saw instead was a line of houses whose windows and doors had been boarded up with plywood; grass grew in front yards as high as his waist with seed heads starting to dry out. Abandoned cars lined the street, some up on blocks and others with at least one flat tire, if they had tires at all. For sure, there were some houses that appeared occupied, but most had tall chain link fences around them, a security feature he had never seen while growing up as a free-range youth. He stopped to look up at the high gable of one of the houses, shading his eyes against the sun.

"Hey! What are you doing?" a voice called from behind him.

He turned to see an older woman sitting in a rocking chair under the porch shade of a house across the street. An alert pit bull crouched beside her. As he crossed the street toward her, the dog shot up and ran at him lunging at the fence and barking viciously.

"Bandit! Bandit!" the woman cried. "Get back here and sit down!"

The dog reluctantly obeyed, looking back over a well-muscled shoulder as it slunk to the porch.

"I used to live on this street," the young man offered. "My family still does. I painted that house when I was in high school. I can still see where I accidentally got some paint on the siding when I was doing the trim work."

"Well, there are precious few of these houses that have been painted since," the lady said.

"Where is everybody?" he asked. "Why are all these houses empty?"

"They're not all empty," the woman said with obvious pride. "Some folks have managed to hang on – mostly because we own our homes outright and because we can't afford to go anywhere else."

He looked at the chain-link fence and the boarded-up houses to either side of the woman's yard.

"You're wondering about the fences and the dog? Well, that's one of the conditions for staying here. The place has been taken over by drug dealers and other vermin. They move from house to house like a pack of rats. I've heard it said that this is the worst zip code in the State of California, and the City's threatened to come in here and just bulldoze the whole neighborhood. The banks own just about everything now – I don't know what they're waiting for."

Mom and Dad never mentioned anything about this in their letters, Don thought. *There was nothing about this in the news we received overseas – even on the internet.* Being in special operations, he knew that a lot of stateside information was filtered for consumption by the troops. Old-timers would have called it censorship for the purpose of morale.

But how could this have happened in just the space of three years? He wondered. *When I left there was an incredible amount of building going on; my dad was superintendent for one of the largest developers in San Diego; my Uncle Kenny had his own contracting company and moved so much dirt that he doubled the number of bulldozers he operated in six months. It seemed that nobody could keep up with the demand for housing.*

Don looked down the street toward where his parents' house stood, about a half block away. The lady on the porch didn't offer any additional information. *He'll have to find out for himself sooner or later,* she thought. *I'm not going to be the bearer of bad news.*

"I've got to go," he said, feeling a sudden sense of urgency. "Excuse me, ma'am."

Don began to walk quickly down the grass-cracked sidewalk, almost breaking into a trot before he got to his parents' place. All along the way, he passed windowless houses with condemnation notices posted like dichotomous welcome signs on their front doors.

His house, unlike most of the others on the block, was not boarded up, but there were *"NO TRESPASSING"* warnings posted in the windows and a couple of placards staked in the front yard like real estate signs that read: *"THIS PROPERTY PROTECTED 24-HOURS BY CENTURY SECURITY!"*

He climbed the steps to the porch. There was a combination padlock attached to a heavy hasp on the front door. Above it, a small plastic sign read: *Property of Bank of America – Call 800-421-2110 for Information.* He felt the blood pressure rise behind his eyes and heard his pulse squeezing through his ear drums. He stepped back away from the door and moved stiffly to look through the front window. Sure enough, the place was empty. It looked like someone had pried out the fireplace mantle and taken the light fixtures, but the wide cherry baseboards and crown molding in the living and dining rooms were still in place. A thin layer of dust covered the oak floors.

Feeling light-headed, Don sat down on the brick-and-concrete banister at the edge of the porch that he and his father had built, his mind emptied by confusion. After a while, he became aware of a sound coming from the back of the house, a sort of rhythmic tinkling that stopped for a few moments then restarted. Leaving his duffle bag, he climbed down the front steps and walked up the driveway cautiously, following the sound which seemed to be coming from the garage. He pushed on the unlocked door and walked in, his eyes taking a few moments to adjust to the darkness.

"Shut the door," a voice said. "Welcome home, Donnie."

"Matt?" he replied, "Is that you?"

"Yep," a disembodied voice replied. "I'm under the truck swapping out a muffler; I'll be with you in a minute. You didn't see any security folks in a white car out there, did you?"

"Nope," Don said, squatting next to the running board of the old Chevy. "Just an old lady down the street with a pit bull."

"That'd be Annie," Matt said. "She's been living there with her sister. Agnes died a few months back. Annie? She'll leave when they carry her out feet first too, I guess."

"What's going on here anyway, Matt? Where's my family?"

"They're all at your Uncle Kenny's up in Ramona. Let me get this finished, and we'll talk on the drive over," Matt replied, grunting as he continued to tighten unseen bolts with his ratchet. "I've gotta get this done quick-like. The druggies usually don't come out until nighttime. But the security folks, well, they can show up any time. I used to stay in the basement of your house until the druggies broke in and stole the mantle and all the light fixtures to sell for meth. That alerted the security pukes, and they nearly caught me instead of the real thieves. When they came down the basement steps, I fired off a few shots from my .22 pistol into the basement walls as I left through the cellar door. I didn't hurt anybody, but it made a lot of noise and sure scared the hell outa those rent-a-cops. They ain't been back here after dark since."

Matt wriggled out from underneath the truck and stood up, dusting off the seat of his pants. Don was about to say something when his friend was alerted to an unseen threat.

"Quick," Matt said. "Get down behind the truck and be quiet. It's one of those security cars creeping up the alley. They'll get to the end and go around to the front to check on the house. When they do, we'll get outa here."

Don heard the light popping of gravel beneath the tires of a car as it passed slowly behind the garage. The driver gunned the engine as the car turned onto the asphalt-paved street at the end of the alley. Matt jumped up quickly, throwing aside the two-by-four brace from the metal brackets on the large swinging garage doors that opened out into the alley.

"Come on. Jump in and let's get the hell outa here."

"I don't much like the idea of running away like a thief from my own house," Don said angrily as he opened the passenger side door and climbed in.

"It's not yours anymore," Matt yelled, throwing the truck into reverse as he backed quickly into the alley, grinding the transmission when he column-shifted into second gear. "It belongs to the Bank of America."

2

By the time the two men turned off eastbound Interstate 8 and headed north on Highway 67 to Ramona, the sun was dusking the west-facing rock formations at the top of Iron Mountain. Don reached down and felt for the door handle. He pushed it forward until he heard the clicking lock that assured he wouldn't fall out of the truck if he leaned against the door. Matt's truck was an old 1955 Chevrolet five-window pickup that he'd bought when they were both seniors in high school. In the first year after graduation, they both had spent a lot of time and money restoring it. Still, one never knew about the integrity of every moving part. That fall, Matt started school at San Diego State. After the World Trade Center attack, Don joined the Marines.

At least this hasn't changed, Don thought as he settled into a familiar cruising position with his knees bent and his feet against the metal dashboard. He had been shocked into silence by their hasty flight from the security patrol but now he wanted answers.

"What in the hell is going on, Matt?" he asked. "Why are my parents at Uncle Kenny's; why does their house have a Bank of America sign on the door?"

"A lot's happened in this country since you went away," Matt replied. "Not much of it any good. It's not going to get much better for a while either."

"I want to know why the neighborhood's gone to hell and why I have to creep around my own house."

"Where do you want me to start?"

"Start somewhere," Don said. "Start talking and don't stop until I tell you."

"About three years ago, in 2008, just about the time you went incommunicado, things went to hell back here in the home building and real estate market," Matt said.

"I wasn't incommunicado; I just couldn't let anyone know where I was or what I was doing for a while," Don replied. "I was part of a very sensitive operation."

"You kill anyone?" Matt asked. "I mean, how many of those ragheads did you dust?"

"Not a one, but I interrogated a shitload of 'em."

"Oh, yeah? Did you water board them like I hear? What is that anyway?"

"No, we didn't torture anyone… just some variations of old Jedi mind tricks."

"Cool. Do you speak Farsi or some such shit? Say something in Arabic."

"You wouldn't understand a word."

"Aw c'mon, just a useful phrase like: 'Take off your burka and let's get friendly.'"

"Okay," Don said:

"رواية
قبل
مايكل هاردينغ"

"Wow! That is too cool. Did you ever get to use a phrase like that?"

"Nope. The women our group interrogated had female handlers, and you didn't want to use that phrase on some guy."

Both young men started laughing. For a moment it was like they were back in high school again, tossing around the rumors about one cheerleader or another. It was Matt who got back to the seriousness of the present situation.

"Everything was going ninety miles an hour when I got out of SDSU. I must have had half a dozen offers to go to work for one company or another, but eventually I went back to work for your Uncle Kenny's contracting group."

"No kidding? We both did that for a year after we graduated from high school. Wasn't that enough for you?"

"It was the times. Your Uncle Kenny is a great guy; he really knows the business. We had all the work we could handle and then some. Did some finish grading for your dad up in the North County. We worked sixty to eighty hours a week... easily. Nobody was complaining, though. People were just snapping up the homes before they were even finished and reselling them... two, maybe three times. Your dad's company finally put a stop to that by requiring buyers to live in the homes for at least a year before they could resell them, but other companies didn't care. Everybody was making money and getting cash bonuses. Now it appears there were more homes built than there were people to live in them because a lot of those houses are empty or only half-built."

"Okay, so that's new housing. But what happened to turn that situation into what I just saw in our old neighborhood?" Don asked.

"Greed and insecurity about the future, I think. The situation seemed too good to be true. Most thought it wasn't going to last very long, so people went nuts borrowing and spending. The government threw fuel on the fire by backing low interest loans to people who really didn't have the resources to make their mortgage payments. I'm not talking about speculative buyers, like me. I'm talking about lower income families who thought this was their only opportunity to own a home. Those folks could buy homes on what the lending agencies called stated income, which doesn't require documentation or much credit history. Sure, it was great at the time. I took out a second mortgage on my house to buy one of the new houses your dad's company was building. I figured that I could flip it in a few years for a profit. Like most loans, it had an adjustable-rate mortgage that ballooned a few years down the road."

"So, what happened?"

"I'm not an economist, but I'll tell you this much. The stock market tanked, and people started getting panicky. The government bailed out Wall Street, banks, and the auto companies because they were 'too big to be allowed to fail,' and credit got tight. With the economic downturn, people started losing their jobs, and they quit buying things, especially houses. It was like one day we were working so hard we couldn't catch our breath, while the next day seemed as if someone knocked the wind out of us.

"Overnight it seemed that home building just stopped. Foundations were half-poured; utilities were stubbed out; entire development phases of subdivisions looked like skeletons of framing material. Your mom lost her teaching job due to state budget cuts, and your dad got laid off. I guess they both figured the housing market was only in a temporary slump or maybe they didn't have a choice. So, like a lot of people, they took out loans on their house to get by in the short term. But there was no short term.

"During the boom times, your Uncle Kenny mortgaged his ranch to buy new construction equipment like bulldozers, graders, and trucks. I guess he'd done it before and had always been able to pay back the notes, even before they became due. He leased me a new four-wheel drive pickup that I drove right up until the day I got laid off. When construction stopped, that truck and that equipment sat idle. The bank eventually took them back and, in the process, called in the note on Kenny's ranch."

"How long of a time period are we talking about?"

"Two years. In my case, one year after I signed the second mortgage on my house, I was out of a job. The payment for the new house I bought doubled with the adjustable interest rate nightmare I was in; renting it out didn't cover half the monthly costs; I couldn't sell the damned thing for even close to what I paid for it. The balloon payment was seventy-five thousand dollars after two years, so I was looking down the barrel of a gun."

"So, in essence, you had two large mortgage payments and no job; but you did have renters in the new house, right?"

"That's right. But the guy living there was a plumber, and he was out of work in a short time as well. So there went that income. The irony is that I was the second owner of that house. The original owner never lived there at all, just bought it on speculation for one hundred fifty thousand. He made a killing when he sold it to me for over two hundred fifty thousand a short time later, while the market was still going up. Great timing for him - just before the slide; not so good for me. I figure that what happened to me must have happened to millions of people across the country as well."

"What did you do?"

"Well, my combined mortgage payments went up to over four thousand a month, so I applied for a new government-backed loan modification program on both houses. To qualify, I was first told I had to make six months of payments without being one minute late. After six months of making those payments on time, I was told to make two payments to the loan company: one for over five thousand and the other for three thousand dollars. They were down payments to secure the refinancing."

"That sounds a little strange."

"It's amazing what you'll agree to do when you're desperate. I was told to send the money by Western Union to a company called Litton Loan. Today, I think that money was just a form of bribe or something similar. Immediately after it was sent off, I received a three-day notice to vacate both properties."

"How is that possible? Was that a legitimate company? Didn't you keep some documentation of this?"

"Sure, I did. I went to college, didn't I? I contacted Litton Loan to ask what was going on, and they said they had never received the funds. I sent them copies of my Western Union receipts with the tracking numbers, but they said it didn't matter because they had already sold the house to Deutsche Bank for one hundred sixty-five thousand dollars. I said that this was a mistake because we were in the middle of a loan modification, and I had complied with all their requirements. A few weeks later, they "found" the five thousand dollars and sent it back to me. As instructed, I resubmitted the payment to Litton by Western Union, and they rescinded the bank sale."

"So, you got to keep the houses?"

"For a time. But it got worse real fast. Everything seemed to be going well on restructuring the loans until I got a statement from Realtime Resolutions who now owned those loans. Litton had taken my money without structuring any modification and turned around and sold the houses to Realtime. Can you imagine? Litton told me to contact Realtime. When I did, Realtime informed me – very arrogantly I might add - that they didn't buy loans to modify them to lower payments."

"Jesus Christ!"

"I have copies of the multiple letters that I wrote to Litton explaining their mistake, but that went nowhere. I once got a letter back that said my money had been placed in a suspense account."

"What in the hell is a suspense account?"

"I have no idea, but I have copies of letters I wrote to them with proof that I had complied with all their requirements and had made my trial payments on time. But that didn't matter for shit; the ball was rolling away from reality and legality. I kept writing letters but got no answers as to why they would take good faith payments and treat a person this way. The money I sent to them was basically stolen from me. I paid for a loan modification that was never delivered."

"If I were to do something like that, I'd be thrown in jail for ten years. It seems corporations like this one have been given a license to steal."

"That's about right," Matt said. "The first mortgage on the house I lived in was to be combined with the second loan into one payment with a lower interest rate. That never happened. The second mortgage was sold back to Litton. If you can believe this, at one point they advised me to stop paying on the first loan to qualify for government mortgage assistance programs. I submitted letters stating that I could pay both mortgages as agreed in the loan modification papers. I never heard anything back from them until they took me to court a year ago for eviction proceedings."

"Sounds like a set up to me."

"I lost the rental and the house that I've lived in for the last three years when it was auctioned to Deutsche Bank for one hundred ninety-seven thousand dollars, a lot less than what I owed on the mortgage. In court, I submitted a letter from Litton stating that, while they disputed the facts that I had presented, they agreed to place my eviction from the house I lived in on hold. The judge agreed with my position but that didn't stop Deustche from filing another lawsuit to evict me from my house. Within a matter of days, I started receiving *cash for keys* letters from a company called Altisource offering relocation help to vacate *their house*."

"Okay. Now who or what in the hell is Altisource?"

"Some offshore company. By now, after nearly two years of fighting, I was whipped. Like a lot of people who bought during the boom, my house had been devalued for loan purposes, and I was, as they say, underwater on my mortgage. I corresponded with Altisource, and they offered me one thousand dollars and one week to vacate. I told them I had been robbed of over eight thousand dollars, and I needed at least a month to get ten years-worth of belongings out of the house. The most disturbing aspect of all was I had to bargain with a company in India for more money and time. The frustration of dealing with an overseas call center was worse than any stress I've ever had in my life."

Don took a deep breath and shook his head. "So, what eventually happened?" he asked.

"That's the kicker. I spoke to a lawyer who said I could sue the bastards because I had all the documentation to make a great case. The problem is that his fees would have been around forty thousand dollars with no guarantee."

"He wouldn't take his fees contingent on winning the case?" Don asked.

"Nope, and he wanted ten thousand as a down payment, too. I figured that if he had only twenty-five percent confidence in winning, then it wasn't worth the chance. It seemed to me like he was just another parasite wanting to make money off a bad situation."

"That's for damn sure."

"So, I figured that it would cost me forty to sixty thousand dollars – which I didn't have anyway – to go to court to save my house. In reality, the most I could hope for was a restructuring of the first and second mortgages. In that case, I would owe over four hundred thousand dollars on a house that had just been auctioned for less than two hundred thousand by Deutsche Bank. I decided to take the fall on this one and start over."

"So, you're basically homeless at this point?" Don said.

"I settled with Altisource for thirty-five hundred dollars, and they gave me one month to vacate," Matt continued. "At the end of that month I left the place in "broom swept condition." A representative came to meet me to exchange the keys for a check. The guy was nice and explained that he too had lost his own home in this nightmare. He said he was super busy with homes all over Southern California, and the person doing the actual cleanup of foreclosed properties was bringing home over ninety thousand a year working for the banks while just installing carbon monoxide detectors and cleaning yards."

"Where did you go after they took back the house?"

"Oh, I've been visiting my friends' abandoned homes in the old neighborhood," Matt laughed. "I dodge the security people during the day and the druggies at night. Just an old ghost, I guess. Some nights I've slipped this old truck into an empty garage to get some sleep, but that's gotten dicey lately because there are a lot of roaming gangs out and about. I still have most of my eviction money in the credit union – not in a bank. I've been eating at the homeless shelters and churches, and it really isn't that bad. I have a locker full of clothes at the YMCA. I clean up there every other day then hit the street looking for work. It's been over a year, but there aren't any jobs."

"Damn," Don said. "It seems to me that if you're a financial corporation in this country you have a license to steal from everyone and get bailed out if being a thief doesn't work out for you."

"That's about it," Matt agreed.

3

As the truck climbed the steep grade of the Old Julian Road, daylight was fading rapidly. When Matt turned into the lane at Uncle Kenny's farm, he needed the headlights for the mile-long drive down the dirt road. When they got to the end of the drive, the house was dark except for the security light out back by the barn. Matt turned off the headlights, and the two men waited while the following road dust cleared from around the truck. Suddenly, Don remembered that his duffle bag was back at his parents' house.

"Dammit! I left my duffle on the porch! Everything I own is in that bag. I guess it'd do no good going back for it now, huh?"

"Consider it gone," Matt said. "If the druggies don't have it, by tomorrow some homeless dude is going to be wearing your underwear for a hat."

Don reached down slowly and tentatively toward the oversized pockets on the lower left leg of his fatigues. His searching fingers identified the outline of his wallet. *Thank God,* he thought, retrieving the billfold, and checking its contents to reassure him that it was still intact. With somewhat more confidence, he unsnapped the pocket on his right thigh and found his discharge papers and checkbook. *Well, that's a positive. I can replace the clothes, but I'll have to figure something out on the gifts I brought back.*

Almost in unison, the two men opened the creaking doors of the old truck and stepped out into the darkness.

"Is that a barbecue I smell?" Don asked.

"I haven't had a good meal for so long I wouldn't know," Matt replied as they cautiously walked through the darkness toward the back yard.

At the rear of the house, they saw a group of children huddled around an open fire near the basketball court. Don's Uncle Kenny was burning steaks on a gas grill. Stopping outside the cone of the mercury vapor light, Matt called out:

"Hey, Uncle Kenny! It's Matt. We're coming in! Don't shoot!"

The conversations around the fire appeared to stop as the four young people gathered there turned to look in their direction. After a few moments of silence, Don heard a familiar voice respond:

"Come on in, boy!" Uncle Kenny called back. "Who's the we? You got a mouse in your pocket?"

Matt and Don moved slowly into the blue light of the mercury vapor lamp, and it was Don's cousin, Paige, standing by the fire who was the first to recognize him. She ran toward them, stopped a few yards short - scuttling some gravel in the process – smiled at Matt, then ran into the house. A few moments later, they heard a screen door slap shut and there, emerging from the shadows of the back porch and taking his place beside his brother Kenny, was Don's dad, Tom. Both men stared in their direction. In the weak light, his father appeared ghostly and much older than the last time Don had seen him. The flash of a sudden grease fire on the grill reflected from his bifocals.

"Damn!" Uncle Kenny said, turning his attention to the grill. "I'm burning my meat!"

"Howdy, Pop!" Don said as he strode over to his father.

Tom Owens moved toward his son, grasped him by the shoulders, and gazed searchingly into his eyes. Then he threw his arms around his son's neck, pulled him to his chest, and began to weep.

After a few awkward moments of silence, Don gently pulled back from his father who turned his face away. The old man pulled a handkerchief from his back pocket and began to absent-mindedly clean his glasses.

"Your mother will be out in a minute," Tom said. "You know how women are. She ran into the bathroom when she heard you were here; reckon she wanted to put her face on or something."

His father had no sooner spoken the words when Elizabeth came into the light drying her hands on her apron, pushing back a few stray strands of hair as she walked purposefully toward her son. In one full motion - absent of any hesitation - she wrapped her arms around him and kissed him hard on his cheek. A small cheer rose from the children as she moved her fingers under his jaw and lightly shook his head in her hands.

"You always knew when it was dinner time," she laughed. "You're welcome to stay, too," she smiled, shooting a quick glance in Matt's direction.

"Thank you, Mrs. Owens," Matt replied. "If it's not too much trouble."

After supper, the children cleaned up by throwing whatever was left over on the open fire. Paper plates, Styrofoam cups, plastic utensils all met the same fate as the children stood in the brief, flared warmth of the blaze, upwind from the toxic smoke. Don and Matt joined Uncle Kenny, Tom, and Elizabeth in the living room by the fireplace in the dim light of flaring oil lamps on the mantle. There wasn't any furniture, so they stood.

"How many of those towel heads did you kill, Donnie?" Uncle Kenny asked.

"None," Don answered. "I was an interrogator; it wasn't part of my job."

"Interrogator?" Uncle Kenny repeated, a surprised look on his face.

"Yeah," Matt added. "But I'll bet he slapped the shit out of a few of 'em."

"That was some feast," Don said, changing the subject. "I haven't had a steak that good in a long time."

"Glad you enjoyed it," Uncle Kenny said, taking a match from a box on the mantle to light his pipe. "I'm afraid we won't be seeing anything like that for a while. That was the last of a prime steer I butchered last fall. What's left in the freezer will go to waste. What a shame."

"What do you mean?" asked Don.

"We've got no electricity," Uncle Kenny said, extending his arm toward the dark recesses of the room. "The utility company shut it off nearly a week ago. Lucky for us we have plenty of propane in the tank and water in the overhead reservoir. We gravity-off the water and heat it with the gas. We've been miserly with both, but it looks like we'll have enough to last through tomorrow. So, we'll be fine."

"What happens tomorrow?" Don asked.

The three older family members exchanged looks between themselves and Matt. It was Tom who was silently elected to explain their situation to Don. Matt already seemed to know.

"You see, son," his father began. "When the construction business started going south a couple of years back, your mother and I had to take out a loan on the house to just keep going. Then, when I lost my job, neither your mother nor I could find decent paying work anywhere. We couldn't keep up the first, let alone the second mortgage payments. After a while, the bank foreclosed on us. That's when we came out here to live with your Uncle Kenny."

"And I wasn't in the best of shape myself," Uncle Kenny added. "My company grew so fast during the housing boom that I mortgaged the ranch to buy more equipment. When everything just stopped and the work dried up, I couldn't find any buyers for the equipment. So that got repossessed, and the loan against this property? Well, I was a few months behind your folks with my predicament, so that gave us all a little time to make some plans."

"They told me the government has programs for people wanting to keep their homes," Matt said, looking toward Don, anticipating the answer he knew was coming.

Uncle Kenny spat into the fireplace.

"That's just political hogwash," Tom said. "We don't know of anyone who qualified or was successful in getting relief. We played a paper game with the banks for over two years, submitting everything they required, three… even four times. In the end they gave us twenty-one days to get out."

"It's like the politicians and bankers repeatedly extended hope but all the while never had the intention of helping people out," Uncle Kenny said. "I think all that paperwork was just a delaying tactic until they arrived at a point that was the most advantageous for them to sell our loans and kick us out."

"Six months ago, the government announced a new program to aid homeowners," Tom added. "The problem was that it applied to no one. To qualify, you had to be current on your mortgage payments, have a good job, and meet standard income-to-debt ratios. Well, Hell's bells. If you met all their criteria, you probably didn't need help!"

"But I hear that interest rates on mortgage loans are at an all-time low, aren't they?" Matt said, chuckling.

"Sure, they are," Uncle Kenny answered angrily. "And so are property values; but just try getting some of that money. The banks aren't making any loans... which really is a bunch of bullshit since it was the taxpayers that bailed them out a few years back. Yep, we were told that the banks were too big to be allowed to fail."

"And we're too small to be of any consequence," Tom added.

"So, what *is* the plan?" Don asked.

"Well, that's the good part," Uncle Kenny said, his eyes appearing to twinkle in the firelight. "Because I was able to hold out a little longer than your folks, the bank offered me five thousand dollars just to quit and get out. I took it. Now, five thousand dollars is not worth a whole lot here in California, but with the money your folks and I have pooled, we bought back part of the old home place in Indiana."

"It's about forty acres on the Flat Rock River in the south-central part of the state," Tom added excitedly. "It was homesteaded by your great-great-grandfather in the mid-1800s. Why, your Uncle Kenny and I used to hunt, fish, and camp along that river when we were boys. It's real dirt, too. We can grow about everything we need to get by, even livestock."

"We've sold off most everything we had of value," Uncle Kenny added. "We figure that if we watch our pennies, we'll have the money to make it there with enough left over to fix up the old house and barn."

"And there's work, too," Tom said. "Maybe not the kind of paying work we've been doing in the last few years but jobs, nonetheless. I don't care if I'm a door greeter at Walmart. A dollar goes a lot further back there than it does out here."

While Uncle Kenny and Tom continued to excitedly discuss all the potential benefits of country living and self-sufficiency in the Midwest,

Elizabeth motioned for Don to join her outside. When he could inconspicuously break away from the man-talk, Don moved out of the light of the fireplace and out onto the front porch. Shortly afterwards, Matt left through the kitchen and out the back door, carefully closing the screen so that it didn't slam shut. All the young people were asleep on bedrolls in the house except for Paige, who waited for Matt behind the barn.

On the porch, Don's mother stood gazing toward the distant lights of Ramona. After a few moments, she took her son's hands into her own, and they sat down on the porch steps.

"Your hands are ice cold, Mom. You ought to get back in the house."

"Was it cold in the desert, Donnie?" she asked, grasping his hands tightly between her own.

"Oh yeah, hot as blazes in the daytime and cold as hell at night."

"I have to ask you something; I've been thinking about it since the day you joined up."

"Go ahead, Mom. We've always talked straight to each other."

Elizabeth took a deep breath and exhaled, the moisture from her breath condensing in the cold night air.

"Did you ever have to kill anybody, Donnie?"

"No, Mom, not directly, anyway. I was an intelligence officer, mostly operating behind the lines. But you know... what we did contributed to the war effort... and people do get killed in war."

"So, you never shot another person?"

"No, there were a lot of guys that needed to be shot... on both sides," he laughed. "But I mainly interrogated them."

In the firelight, Don could see the relief on his mother's face.

"Good. I always felt like taking someone else's life would make a person cruel and mad, have them lose all compassion for their fellow human beings. You haven't lost your respect for life, have you Donnie? You're still my same sweet boy, aren't you?"

"Sure, I am. There's no need for you to worry."

"The time for being mad is behind this family now. Your father and I are just exhausted from being angry all the time. The family's looking ahead to a new beginning back where we came from. Your father and Uncle Kenny were beat down for a while, but once they began to focus on a different future, things changed. They're all right now."

"And you, Mom? Are you alright?"

"I'm fine. I've still got your brother and sisters to raise regardless of where we are."

"What about your career, Mom? Aren't you mad about all the years you put into teaching being lost?"

"They're not lost, Donnie. Never lost. More like remembered than lost. Besides, who knows what I might be able to do back in Indiana?"

"Well, I'd be pissed."

"I'm not saying for you not to be mad, Donnie; just don't put it away somewhere where it fumes and festers into some wrathful eruption. I need you to turn your anger into positive action and help me get this family across the country and started up again. You are going with us, aren't you?"

"Sure, Mom, I'll help out any way I can."

"I'm so sorry you had to come back to this Donnie."

"You don't have to apologize to anyone Mom, least of all, me. I just don't understand why you didn't let me know about this."

"Your father and I didn't think it was going to end up like this. We always thought that we'd pull out of it somehow. When it became apparent that we were going to lose the house, it was just too uncomfortable to talk about."

"I might've done something."

"I don't know what that would've been. Besides, we didn't want to burden you, what with the situation you were in over there."

They heard the back-door screen door creak open, and slam shut, and they both looked in the direction of the sound.

"We'll talk no more about this. You better get some sleep; it'll be a long day tomorrow. There are some extra bed rolls in the trailer; you and Matt can sleep there tonight if you'd like."

Elizabeth kissed her son on the cheek as she stood. She moved across the porch past the weakly illuminated windows and into the darkness of the house.

Paige entered the side door of the old hipped-roof barn and lit the kerosene lantern hanging on the wall. Her father's shop was empty except for a few ancient hand tools on the work bench that were left over from the sale. On the floor was a monkey wrench, and she picked it up. Attempting to turn the handle-nut to adjust the jaws, she realized it was broken: *Probably the reason it had not sold at the auction,* she thought.

Matt entered the room quietly, closed the door behind him and watched as Paige worked to loosen the jaws of the wrench. She turned toward him, dropping the tool to the dirt floor. They quickly embraced; he, encircling his arms around her waist, and she, placing her hands against his chest, resting her head between them, bending her body against his as they shared a long and passionate kiss.

Dropping his hands to her thighs, Matt gently lifted her to a sitting position on the work bench and parted her knees, moving between them. Without losing contact with his mouth, Paige wrapped her legs around his hips, entwined her fingers around his neck and pulled him hard against her. In a few moments, they began the slow, sensual undulations that initiate lovemaking. But when Matt attempted to unbutton her blouse, Paige pulled away, breathing heavily.

"No," she said between short gasps. "Not now, not here. We need to wait."

"Wait for what?" he said, lightly groaning with a familiar frustration.

"I want our first time to be special. Not here, not in a barn, not when we're leaving tomorrow morning. I don't know when I'll see you again!"

"There never has been a good time," he said, calmly unlocking himself from her embrace and moving out of the lantern light and toward the door.

"I love you," she cried after him.

"And I love you," he replied, stepping out into the darkness.

4

The exodus began as a trickle almost a decade before the housing bubble burst in 2008. As home values appreciated in the first decade of the millennium, a few people in California began to cash out and take their inflated equity to other states where property values and the cost of living were lower. A family could sell their home in San Diego for more than twice what they owed on it, take the profit, and pay cash for property somewhere else. One summer, for nearly a month, articles ran in the San Diego Union Tribune - testimonials of a sort - from folks that had moved away to Chickasha, Oklahoma or Seattle, Washington boasting of a new life unfettered by mortgages, unconstrained by traffic congestion, free of the tedium of perpetual sunny days, and the monotony of unchanging seasons.

In the beginning Californians headed north along the coast to Oregon and Washington State, but as a result bargain prices for real estate in those areas didn't last very long. The local populations - especially the Oregonians - became resentful of the invaders because the economic immigration caused an increase in the price of housing in Bend, Eugene, Portland, and other towns throughout the state. If one already owned property in these areas, well, that wasn't so bad because your home was worth more overnight. But if you were hoping to buy a house or a few acres of land on which to build your retirement dream, then you were probably priced out of the market as the demand for these parcels increased, and so consequently their value.

Americans have always been - by both nature and history – a nation of immigrants, adapting their dreams to fit the character of their environment. In the early settlement years of the continent, those dreams appeared as limitless as the waves of immigrants surging into the western wilderness beyond the Alleghenies. Once the margin of the Pacific Ocean was reached, the backrush of civilization into the interior established boundaries to that ambition - and the borderlines were comprised of ownership and privilege. Those that got there first took possession of the land. Over time, that tenure resulted in contempt toward those who came afterwards to fill the unoccupied areas on the perimeter of the landowners' entitlements.

Less than two hundred years after Lewis and Clark reached the Pacific, the first wave of "Californicators" settled into their new life among the lush pastures and rainforests of the Northwest Territory, swelling the roads with their rust-free BMWs and Mercedes, reveling in the cool, moist air and rainfall on their paling, upturned faces. As Eddie Bauer stores took the place of Saks Fifth Avenue and Nordstrom, the ex-pats discovered khaki pants and plaid shirts, sweater-vests, windbreakers, waterproofs, and micro-breweries. They adapted to the change from a dry to a damp environment. After a few years, it was hard to tell the natives from the newcomers who had, over time, developed a latter-day contempt for more recent arrivals from the Golden State: "We're being overrun by Californians!" they cried, avoiding mirrors like vampires.

But there was no void left in California from the exodus, for any temporal vacuum was immediately filled by the influx of international immigrants from Mexico, Central and South America, Southeast Asia, and Central Europe. Bilingualism had long been practiced in the public-school system as the region had been Spanish California long before it came into the possession of the English-speaking United States. In the decade of the 1990s, social service bulletins dealing with everything from public safety to storm water pollution prevention were reproduced in English, Spanish, Mandarin, Russian, and Vietnamese. Signs regulating fishing in Santa Monica Bay were printed in Hmong. And though most people in California thought of the growing diversity as cultural enrichment, here again the ugly specter of time-honored privilege and prerogative fought against the dreams and aspirations of the newly arrived.

The United States – and California – has become a giant lending library of cultures. As one book is checked out another is returned. And although they may not be of the same subject and character, all books – whether they are hardcover or paperback, comprised of a set or a single volume – enrich the overall collection from which we are all free to borrow.

Americans stampeded to the Oklahoma Territory in 1889 to acquire free land from the government. Less than fifty years later, their children were pretty much stampeded out of the state, driven by unrelenting drought, crop failure, consolidation of agricultural production, and land ownership by the banks. Most did not own the farms that they sharecropped, but they had cultivated an agrarian connection to the dusty land and nurtured a blood-fertilized investment that went back generations. The "Okies" flight from the Dust Bowl and drought of the "Thirties" toward the greener pastures and orchards of California was a mass movement of culture; each person, every family, shared common traits of hard-scrabble industry and self-reliance, of jaw-clenching humility, and despair. The hordes moved as if driven by the invisible blade of a Caterpillar tractor, tumbling over and over from one Hooverville to the next, unable to put down roots and grow strong in the well-watered valleys of the West. Their strength was in their numbers and numbers nurtured inevitability. Californians already established in their homes and businesses knew this and looked on these denim-shadowed human beings as they might a plague of locusts.

Farmers and businessmen grew leery of the power of this displaced population as well they should have, for common values and shared suffering forge a kinship sometimes greater than blood. Around the campfires along roadsides and beside the cooking fires in Hoovervilles at the outskirts of towns, lean, strong, desperate men talked treason, not subversion of a government but the overthrow of a system that – in a land of plenty - allowed a few to benefit while fertile land was left fallow, and their families withered on slave wages. A commonality of poverty and purpose connected each family to the other. It was only through the benevolent absence of a readily identifiable body on which to fasten their misery that they didn't rise up with pitchforks, scythes, and axe handles to vent their parched anger.

There are some similarities between the Dust Bowl Oklahomans and the Twenty-First Century's economic emigration of Californians, but there are just as many differences. First, after the initial dribble of fortune seekers to the Pacific Northwest, the movement of the vast majority of the dispossessed and homeless during the second decade of the new millennium was along the fabled Route 66 – now for the most part an interstate highway - but in the opposite direction, west-to-east. These modern Bedouins traveled in better vehicles with more comfort than the "Okies." Most had an idea of where they were heading and what awaited them at the end of their journey: a new job, relatives who could put them up until they got settled, and government support systems that allowed them to collect unemployment wherever they ended up.

The new immigrants also travelled more quickly and, for the most part, individually or as a family unit. Although they might share a common campground with other nomads, they did not share their stories around campfires or happily join in choruses of impromptu singing. They were suspicious and wary of other transients. Theirs was a flight of economic embarrassment, from domestic dreams that had ruptured against the strain of unemployment and the hard falseness of the American dream. They no longer believed that everyone should be able to own a home or that their children would prosper and someday accomplish more than their parents. By and large they were a more educated and intelligent group of itinerants. In being so, they understood more fully the circumstance of their desolation. The country would take a long time to recover, and they would probably die without property to pass on to a generation burdened with unimaginable debt.

What the new migrants shared with the Oklahomans, however, was a seething sense of anger and betrayal. Theirs was an unshakeable belief that the source of their misery dwelled in Washington, D.C. and that succubus was sustained by politicians in general. It was as if the ancient Okies – nearly all of them dead and planted in the fertile ground of California's valleys – had sprouted a new generation of plant life, more articulate, politically aware, and possessed with a residual, tactile memory of what it was like to heft a pitchfork, a scythe, or an axe handle.

5

By the time the sun rose above the Cuyamaca Mountains to the east, all the Owens family vehicles that were to make the trek back to Indiana were packed. The four adult men had gotten up at the crack of dawn to load the heavier items while the younger members of the group brought out their bedrolls, pre-packed suitcases and duffels, the quantity of which was limited by their parents and by necessity.

The adults took very little themselves. Most of the hardware and appliances from the house in San Diego and the ranch in Ramona had been sold or auctioned off weeks before. Valuable papers and precious items - like jewelry and family keepsakes - had been sent by insured mail to a cousin in Indianapolis who promised to hold them until the family got settled on their river property.

The inventory of that eastbound wagon train consisted of two older pickup trucks, both with extended cabs, purchased through the sale and trade of the families' previously owned vehicles. The men had installed low, locking fiberglass shells that covered the bed of each truck to protect the items packed tightly underneath. Tom, Elizabeth, and their children - the seventeen-year-old twins, Jenny and Julie, and their thirteen-year-old brother, Scout, were to ride in a Ford F-250 that towed a pop-up camper trailer. Don's cousin, Paige, who was twenty-one, rode with her father in the other pickup. At bedtime, all the girls were to share the privacy of the tent camper with Elizabeth. The men planned on sleeping in the back-seat cab of each truck while Scout would make his bed across the front seat of the truck driven by his father. This was all well thought out in advance, and the sleeping arrangements were not only comfortable but provided a certain level of security for the people and items that were to be transported nearly two thousand miles.

Kenny's truck had dual tires on the rear axle and pulled an old but sturdy silver Airstream trailer that had been stripped down to serve its basic function of providing a place to clean up and to cook. The beds had been taken out to make room for the taller furniture that had been in the family for generations and could not be sold. There was a small stove and refrigerator powered by two propane gas tanks strapped to the front hitch. Once in Indiana, the Airstream would supply additional living space while the house was being restored and retrofitted to accommodate the two families.

The adults had determined to take no more than a week to make the crossing – about four hundred miles a day. They had calculated the route, the distance, the optimum speed for economical fuel consumption, where the rest stops were located, and what tourist sites could be visited along the way without getting too much off their route of travel. Most importantly, they searched the web for locations of Walmarts along the way, in part because the stores were where they expected to provision their little expedition but also because they planned to park overnight in the expansive parking lots. Uncle Kenny had heard that Walmart welcomed such visitors and had even opened a new department in each store to accommodate the twelve-volt needs of the recreational vehicle public.

That morning, there was a high level of excited expectation among the teenagers. Elizabeth put the twin girls and Scout to work polishing the aluminum of the Airstream. *Best for them to burn off some energy,* she thought. *It's going to be a long trip.* She instructed the twins on how to apply the polish, let it dry, and use a cloth to buff the metal. She gave Scout the responsibility of cleaning the windows of the trucks and told him that this would be his chore – to be completed every morning before breakfast - and he appeared happy with the job.

Julie and Jenny were less than thrilled by the prospect of the journey. They were to start their senior year at Patrick Henry High School. The twins tried not to imagine the social horrors that awaited them at their new rural school.

Paige had been attending Grossmont College for the last two years with the goal of enrolling at the University of California in Berkeley, but now, that was economically out of the question. She would probably have to settle for a community college somewhere close to the farm until she could gain residence status and attend Indiana University in Bloomington. Her goal was to become a journalist, and she considered chronicling the family's odyssey across the country. But being uprooted from her life in San Diego had left her too heartbroken to begin the effort. *If Matt were to come along*, she thought, *well, that would make a big difference.*

As the children set about their assigned tasks, Tom and Kenny stood on the front porch and sipped at their coffee in the new morning chill. Don and Matt were busy sweeping the floors of the house while Elizabeth went from room to room checking to make sure nothing important was left behind. Paige was removing the bulbs from the overhead light fixtures. After the last room was broomed out, Don and Matt joined the two older men on the porch.

"I imagine it'll take longer to unload it all once we get there," said Tom, arching his back, his hands on his hips.

"That's if we only have the two of us to unload," said Uncle Kenny. "You're coming aren't you, Donnie?"

"Well, I thought I might... just to make sure you all get there safely. After that, I'm not exactly sure what I want to do."

"What about you, Matt?" Tom asked. "You wanna come along?"

"I'd sure like to," Matt replied, looking toward the house. "Got nothing holding me back, and there's a lot of ground between here and Indiana I've never seen. I'll bring my truck. Donnie... you can ride with me if you'd like."

"I'll start out with you," Don suggested. "That way I'll be available to spell the other drivers when they need a break. And since I'm the only one not supplying a vehicle, I'll buy the gas for your truck."

"Sounds fair to me," Matt said.

In front of them a dust cloud was rising from the dirt lane as a car made its way toward the house.

"Right on time," Uncle Kenny announced. "Eight-thirty, on the dot!"

The driver stopped a respectful distance from the house so that the dust did not reach the people standing on the porch. After a few seconds, a young man in a suit got out of the car and walked toward the house carrying a manila envelope. He approached the porch where the family was standing but didn't climb the steps to join them. Instead, he extended the envelope toward Uncle Kenny who accepted it and tucked it under his arm.

"Chris!" Don exclaimed. "What are you doing here? I haven't seen you since basic training."

"Hello, Donnie," Chris replied. "I heard you were back."

"You shouldn't be serving papers on your friends," Matt said darkly, "and kicking them off their property!"

"What the hell's going on here, Chris?" Don asked.

"Now, boys," Uncle Kenny said softly. "These aren't eviction papers." He held out the manila envelope so Don could examine it. "Chris just brought us the settlement check from the bank, the papers we got a while back."

"I'm sorry fellas," Chris said. "I don't like it much, but it's a job. My parents lost their home too, and they live with me and the wife now."

"That's okay, son," Tom offered. "We don't blame you; besides, we're kind of looking forward to getting on the road to a new beginning. We've got prospects."

"And good luck to you on that, really," Chris responded. "So many of the families I've had to face have fallen apart, gone in different directions or just don't know what to do. From what you've told me, I think you'll make it just fine and probably come out ahead in the end."

"We aim to," said Elizabeth, who suddenly appeared on the porch. "Hello, Chris! She's all swept out and ready to go."

"Thank you, Mrs. Owens," Chris replied. "Donnie, I've got something for you in the trunk."

Surprised, Don climbed down from the porch and joined Chris as he moved to the back of the car. Chris opened the trunk and pulled out Don's duffel bag.

"Well, I'll be damned!" Don exclaimed. "How'd you get this?"

"Those security guys are friends of mine," Chris explained. "We served in the same unit in Iraq. They brought it into the bank last night. Cool, huh?"

"They'd have arrested me if they'd caught me," Don said angrily. "At my own house."

"Look man," Chris said. "They're not bad guys; everybody's just trying to survive. When those guys were sent home and discharged, there were no jobs for them. They've got families; what can you do?"

"There's a lot more men that'll be coming back to this mess," Don said. "The government's downsizing the military; you know that. Those guys are gonna be pissed. What's gonna happen then?"

"I don't know," Chris said extending his hand. "They'll try to survive, I guess. Unless there's another war to fight, I can't see the situation getting much better for a while. Your family's got the right idea; get out of here and go back to a place where it's easier to live. I think about the folks I've met that are trapped in a mindset that doesn't allow them to think of any other possibility than to stay where they are and just wither."

Don shouldered his duffel and shook his friend's hand, noticing that Chris's eyes had started to mist over.

"Good luck to you, man," Don said, "Semper Fi."

Chris opened the door to the car, climbed in, and prepared to leave. As he rolled down the window and waved, Elizabeth called out to him:

"You'll tell your folks we said goodbye, won't you Chris?"

"I sure will, Mrs. Owens," he shouted back. "Good luck! God bless all of you!"

6

In the last year leading up to their departure from California, as they waited for the next shoe to drop, the older members of the Owens family - Ken, Tom, and Elizabeth - had felt listless, useless, and mostly ashamed that they had let their children down. The fact that many of their neighbors and business associates in the construction community were suffering in similar circumstances provided little comfort.

For a while, when there was still some work to be had, Tom and Ken attended the monthly meetings of the Engineering and General Contractors Association out of a sense of shared obligation and the desperate hope that they might scare up a little business. Men who had always been able provide for their families – hard bitten contractors that had weathered the competitive winds and occasional slumps of the industry in their younger years – were now in their late fifties or older and less elastic. Each put on a brave face in front of their peers, but behind their eyes panic grew. As the construction drought dragged on and business bankruptcies became more commonplace, the attendance at these meetings started to lag. For those that did show up, conversation around the dinner tables spiraled downward from general bitch sessions to almost no conversation at all. When the rotating get-togethers became bi-monthly and had to be held in someone's shop instead of a nice restaurant, the Owens brothers quit going. It was just as well; they couldn't afford the cost of the meal let alone the bar tab.

When members of the construction community bumped into each other on the street, at a school function, or in a local tavern, the discussions that ensued were not what a person outside the business would ever expect. Conversations never started with: "Remember when..." or "Back in my day..." Contractors and builders are born optimists; that's just the way it is. If you don't have self-confidence and a positive outlook, then construction – and farming for that matter

- is not the business for you. One other shared characteristic is patriotism and love of country. Many of them had served in the military and almost all of them voluntarily.

For that reason alone, contractors are for the most part, politically conservative, Republican, and capitalists. When market forces descended on their businesses and way of life, it became necessary to find someone to blame. Bankers, state government, politicians, Wall Street, foreign competition, immigration, and Al Qaeda all took their turn on the great rotating wheel of denunciation. But their supreme indictment was reserved for the so-called environmentalists. They - whoever "they" were - blocked development with endangered species, obstructed progress by introducing new rules and regulations, slowed local agency building approvals through a lengthy permit process, and generally added additional costs to the way business was traditionally conducted.

In truth, there was probably enough blame to apportion everyone a share of responsibility for the collapse, although none of the participants would want to admit that their interests had anything to do with it. Democrats blamed the previous Republican administration; Republicans blamed the current Democratic President; banks blamed market forces while Wall Street kept rolling along on its typical symbiosis of speculation and greed. For anyone who had an above-average understanding of the mortgage business, a special hell was reserved for speculators that bundled toxic mortgages and sold them for a profit.

California has long been a trend setter for the nation in general. Although the East Coast cities of New York, Boston, and Washington, D.C. might be the focal point for publishing, sports, and old-style politics, Los Angeles and Southern California in general have always spoken to a younger audience through art, music, and political activism. People in the middle of the country share a perception that the climate out West is virtually unchanged from summer through winter. Californians are generally a lazy lot, spending their days at the beach and their nights partying under balmy breezes. Movies and television expand this impression across the nation; that it's always sunny in California and that its people are beautiful, economically advantaged, and largely made up of idlers or the homeless. Of course, nothing could be further from the truth unless one is talking about the State Legislature.

In the decade before the great collapse, Sacramento politics raised partisanship to new heights never seen in other states. State Representatives and Senators were so impotent at getting meaningful legislation enacted that they had to resort to a system in which the entire state voted through direct initiative processes called propositions or referendums at election time, issues that their elected representatives should have addressed in the legislature. Some thought that the proposition procedure empowered the constituency, but in fact, actual political influence was illusory.

As California pivots, so does the nation, and it was unfortunate that in the years of economic downturn following the collapse of the building industry, national politics in Washington began to mirror those in Sacramento. Partisanship in the houses of Congress engendered bitterness and intransigence on both sides of the aisle. Meanwhile, relief for the unemployed, help for people whose homes were being taken from them, even a generally acknowledged need for universal health care, became politicized to the point of exhaustion. The Owens family – and others like them – became the trampled vintage of unrealized promise through the inaction of politicians who lacked a sense of common purpose to move the country forward.

7

By the time the caravan left Ramona and headed east on Interstate 8, the sun had already risen to an angle above the roof line of each truck so that the drivers were not irritated by the direct early morning rays. But as the vehicles descended through the bouldered banks of the Mountain Springs' grade, the harsh white light seemed to skip off the desert floor and ricochet around the interior of the cabs causing them to warm up, seemingly from friction.

There were yellow warning signs for the steepness of the grade – about a six percent decline – and other signs for the high winds that scoured the passes and occasionally flipped over the box trailer of a big rig, but this morning - with Tom in the lead pulling the Airstream trailer - everyone stayed in low gear, never topping thirty-five miles an hour as they coasted the undulating ten mile stretch of bleached asphalt. The weather was cool; the winds were calm; the trucks didn't overheat. The strong winds came later in the day.

Bringing up the rear of the string, Matt and Don had comfortably settled into conversation, catching up on each other's activities after years of operating in different spheres.

"So," Matt began. "As an interrogator, did you ever get involved in any of that torture stuff we heard about a few years back. I mean, is it okay to ask you questions about that?"

"There's really nothing to talk about. Most of what I did was pretty mundane; that is to say, we had a routine where if someone brought in a prisoner it was our job to ask them some questions to determine what the next level of processing would be."

"For instance?"

"Well, in most cases, particularly in Iraq, most of the people I interviewed were just normal folks. We were set up in the outskirts of the cities, and we processed candidates for the new Iraqi Army or the home police force. The idea was to make sure that we didn't have any former Baath Party members in positions of authority; that was Saddam Hussein's former political group."

"How did that work out?"

"Not always very well. First, the Baathists were the ones who knew how to run everything - from the bureaucracy to the power plants. So, putting inexperienced people in their places created some problems for a while. If you ever saw the scene in *Lawrence of Arabia* when the Bedouin Army arrives in Damascus and Omar Sharif tries to get everyone organized - you'll understand what I mean. It was chaos. I love that movie."

"Inexperience is one thing, but could you trust the ones that you screened?" Matt asked.

"For the most part, yes," Don answered. "But a determined Jihadist will always find a way. I'm sure you've heard stories about local security headquarters being attacked and police candidates being killed by fellow officers."

"Oh, yeah," Matt said. "Wasn't there even a U.S. Army officer – a Muslim - that took out some troops at Fort Hood, Texas?"

"Yep, so, you can imagine how difficult the situation was working in-country. Shortly after that incident, I got transferred to Afghanistan."

"How was that different?" Matt asked.

"Not much, except at first, I was mainly dealing with illiterate villagers. You develop sympathy for the way they've been squeezed between the government, the Taliban, tribal chiefs, and the U.S. Military. They either seem scared all the time or pissed off."

"Did you ever see any Taliban?"

Don took a deep breath, controlled his exhalation, and looked out the side window across the desert before he answered.

"I was called in on a couple of interrogations. I was there to report back to my commander on the methods that were used and whether or not they were effective."

"What kind of methods are we talking about?"

"Not what you'd expect. Mainly sleep deprivation; having the dudes stand for hours on end with their arms extended, playing heavy metal music over and over."

"There were photos on the web that showed a naked guy."

"Nudity is all part of the deal. It's especially humiliating to Muslims, which is really the whole purpose of the exercise. There's really no physical torture - just some form of Jedi mind tricks. That is, except for the waterboarding; I guess you could call that physical torture."

"Waterboarding? How does that work?"

"They would strap a naked guy down on a wooden plank, cover his face with a cloth, and position him so that his feet were higher than his head. Then they'd drip water on the cloth for around ten seconds or until he started to choke. The process would be repeated over and over. They claim that the procedure simulates the effects of drowning."

"Did it work? Did they break down and talk?"

"Oh, yeah. After a few weeks of this type of treatment even the most hardened man would be willing to give up some information. That's when they were taken somewhere else for further interrogation by the CIA or FBI. I had nothing to do with them after that."

"Do you think it did any good?"

"I'm told that some of the information acquired in this manner – especially right after the attack on the World Trade Center - foiled a lot of terrorist plots worldwide and especially some homegrown activities here in the United States."

"Do you think that's true?"

"I'd like to think so, but I can't be certain."

Matt waited a few minutes before asking his next question:

"Do you have any regrets about participating in those interrogations?"

"Not at all. One of the guys that I watched being interrogated was the asshole that slit a reporter's throat right on camera and sent the video out for the world to see. I figure that he was treated pretty gently by comparison."

"So why did you leave the service?"

"I have no regrets; I just didn't want to see that anymore; I got tired of watching human beings degraded and debased, innocent or guilty."

The two men drove in silence for a few miles, the whine of the old truck's tires punctuated with a rhythmic thud caused by the concrete road joints.

"So, I asked for my discharge, intending to come back home to decency and compassion," Don said, gritting his teeth. "And what do I find within twenty-four hours? That the simple security of having a job and home is gone; that the trust between Americans and the institutions of government and business has been betrayed; that my family has been robbed of their dignity and put out on the road. What the hell was I fighting for?"

"To put a stop to terrorism," Matt answered. "That's what I always heard."

"Maybe," Don said. "But I think the terrorists have already won."

8

The first planned stop for the group was Yuma, Arizona. The caravan arrived together at a Shell station on the south side of the Colorado River that had the best price on gasoline. While the men filled up the fuel tanks of the trucks and checked the oil levels, Paige recorded the mileage they had traveled by reading each odometer and collecting the gas receipts to determine the miles per gallon for each vehicle. Her aunt had instructed her to keep track of the times of the trip as well. Elizabeth's intent was to assign the young people tasks that would engage their minds and keep them focused more on what was ahead rather than what they were leaving behind. Meeting his responsibility, Scout climbed onto the running boards to clean the windshields of the trucks with the squeegees and paper towels provided by the service station.

"Almost exactly three hours from Ramona to Yuma," Paige announced to her father. "Eleven point six-six gallons; that's about fifteen miles to the gallon, Uncle Tommy. Daddy, you took fourteen point three-five gallons for one hundred seventy-five miles; that's twelve point two-four miles per gallon. It's not quite as good, but that's probably because we have a larger engine and pulling the bigger trailer."

"What was our average speed?" her Aunt Elizabeth asked, always the teacher.

"About fifty-eight miles an hour," she estimated. After pressing a few keys on her hand-held calculator, she smiled: "Yes, fifty-eight point three miles an hour to be exact!"

"Girls!" Elizabeth called to the twins. "Would you please get the cooler out of the back of the truck and bring it over to the picnic table? Everyone use the bathroom and wash your hands; we'll have our lunch here before we start down the road again."

"You don't want to just eat as we go?" Tom asked. "That'd save some time, wouldn't it?"

"Heavens, no!" Elizabeth replied. "We need to let these children stretch their legs a bit. We're not in that big of a hurry, are we? We can be a little civilized about this, too! Matt! Don! You wash up, too!"

A picnic table was located on a piece of sloping dirt, off the pavement and near the twenty-five-cent air compressor. There was no shade, and the day had already begun to heat up. The four children crowded onto one side of the bench, and Elizabeth, Tom, and Uncle Kenny took up positions on the other side. Matt backed his truck to the edge of the curb and dropped the tailgate. Paige got up from the picnic table, retrieved three sandwiches from Elizabeth, and joined Matt at the rear of the truck.

"Where's Donnie?" Uncle Kenny asked.

"He's inside getting some cold sodas for everyone," Matt said.

"There's no need for him to do that," Elizabeth said. "We've got drinking water in the cooler."

"I think he just wanted to treat the kids," Tom said, smiling at his wife. "No harm in that, is there honey? We can be a little civilized about this, can't we?"

Elizabeth continued to hand out the baloney sandwiches without looking at her husband. "I just don't want to stop every twenty miles because someone has to go to the bathroom. We're going, so let's just keep going."

"You think we can make Flagstaff by this evening, Uncle Tommy?" Paige asked.

"With the rate we're going," her uncle answered, "we should get there before dark; that's if we don't have to stop to pee every twenty miles!"

Everyone laughed, including Elizabeth.

Inside the convenience store, Don was paying for the Chevy's fuel. He picked up a six pack of Mountain Dew and another of Diet Coke, placing them near the cash register.

"I have a few more things to get," he told the attendant, and started down the aisle to pick out candy bars for his siblings and some corn nuts and other treats for the adults. He pulled the front of his t-shirt out at the waist to carry his road food selections. When it was bulging, he proceeded back to the counter where two small Mexican children, each clutching a bag of M & M's, offered a dollar bill to the cashier.

"Them candies is a dollar each," the cashier said, clearly irritated and anxious to ring up Don's larger sale. "That's two dollars."

She held out her hand toward the children, bending her fingers back against her palm in a grasping motion.

The boy placed the dollar bill on the counter while his little sister waited, wide-eyed.

"Two dollars," the lady said. *"Dos!"*

"You know," Don said, winking at the cashier. "I think those candies were two for a dollar."

The woman looked toward Don with an air of surprise then flashed a harder look at the children.

"Vamoose!" she said, slipping the offered dollar into the pocket of her apron as the children instantly ran out of the store clutching their candy, disappearing into the dark interior of an old station wagon. As she began to ring up his purchases, Don watched the rusted-out car - weighed down by an excess of furniture and personal possessions tied onto the roof with twine - ease out of the gas station and head west toward California.

"They'll steal you blind if you let 'em!" she said to Don, expecting his affirmation.

"Just ring it up," he replied, coldly. "Plus, one dollar."

9

Three hours and one hundred eighty miles later, the caravan pulled into a service station in the suburb of Surprise, just west of Phoenix, Arizona. They had been delayed only once for a bathroom break at a roadside rest stop. The twins had held out tenaciously, and Scout resolutely retained his Mountain Dew for nearly an hour. But when Paige - in the lead truck - spotted the blue sign that said: *Rest Stop – 2 Miles* - everyone obtained relief and Elizabeth achieved vindication.

With Flagstaff a mere two hours up the road and the sun still high above the horizon, the little group proceeded onward. Elizabeth admonished everyone to get out their jackets.

"It'll be colder as we get into the mountains. Flagstaff is over seven thousand feet in elevation, and it'll probably be dark by the time we arrive."

This bit of information stirred excitement in the teenagers' minds. *That's twice as high as the Cuyamacas,* Jenny thought, looking toward her twin. *I wonder if there's snow.* Julie answered back without giving voice to her thoughts. *Bears*, Scout thought. *Grizzly bears and mountain goats.* He visualized the bleaching bones of ancient prospectors strewn among the rocks, guarding the crumbling portals of their gold mines like pirates. Paige was thinking about Matt.

By the time Uncle Kenny and Paige led the family wagon train into the Walmart parking lot across from the Northern Arizona University campus, there were already recreational vehicles of all types encamped in the southern portion of the expansive paved area. In addition to the standard, boxy-looking diesel-pushers, there were over-the-road big rigs with living quarters behind the driver's cab the size of a small bedroom; vans with pop-tops, trucks with camper shells and simply cars with all a family's belongings strapped to the hoods or bulging out of overstuffed trunks. There seemed to be an unwritten rule that the emigrant ephemera was obligated to locate itself as far away as possible from the front doors of the store so as not to impede the paying customers.

Most of the occupants of these vehicles were assembled in small social knots centered around gas-fired grills where the evening's supper had already been or was in the process of being cooked and eaten. There was a scattering of cheap, collapsible chairs constructed of tubular aluminum and nylon fabric of various colors – most with cup holders in the arms. And there were a few folding tables of dull aluminum or white plastic placed end-to-end on which it appeared that a spare but communal feast had been laid.

Uncle Kenny drove slowly down one of the open traffic lanes past this transient community. The children within the groups appeared inquisitive, but the adults looked listless, apathetic, and road weary. In a less occupied area of the parking lot, the family found adjacent spaces that would accommodate both trucks and trailers and provide for an easy exit in the morning. Tom followed Uncle Kenny and parked parallel alongside. By the time Matt and Don arrived, Tom was already at the door of the Airstream directing the removal of the family's folding furniture, and Elizabeth was supervising their placement by the children. Matt parked the Chevy next to the family area but only pulled halfway through the adjoining spaces, straddling them in the middle.

"Everyone go inside, and use the bathrooms and wash your hands," Elizabeth commanded. "Tom, you go buy three of those roasted chickens along with some coleslaw and potato salad. We've got paper plates and napkins, but I can't find the paper cups. You might get a sleeve of them and a half gallon of milk for the children."

"Let's go kids," Tom called, and he and Uncle Kenny shepherded the children up an adjacent aisle less occupied than the one they had just come down. Unspoken was the brothers' impression that the groups they had passed appeared to be somewhat desperate and needy.

"We'll be back after a while, so don't wait supper on us," Don said to his mother. "Matt left his stuff back at the YMCA. Outside of what I have on, everything in my duffle is military. We need some clothes."

"Yeah," added Matt. "We need some civvies and some toiletries, as it were. My clothes are starting to develop a life of their own."

"Mom," Don asked. "You reckon if Matt and I get an air mattress that it could ride in the Airstream? We'll sleep in the back of the Chevy, but I figure it'll blow out if we try to carry it in the truck bed during the day."

"That'll be just fine. Would you boys mind raising the pop-up before you go? I'll show you how; it'll only take a minute. That way it will be done before dark."

"Sure, Mrs. Owens," Matt replied. "We were talking about heading into town or over to the college a little later."

Boys will be boys, Elizabeth thought and smiled inwardly. She considered saying something like: *Watch yourselves* or *be careful!* But they were adults now and Don had done a lot of growing up in the military. Instead, she just said: "Have fun!" Paige thought otherwise.

After buying toiletries, underwear, socks, t-shirts, and a couple of pairs of jeans apiece, Matt and Don completed their shopping spree in the Walmart with the purchase of the queen-sized air mattress and a large tarp with elastic ties to extend over the truck bed in case it rained. After stowing the items in the Airstream and changing into some of their new clothes, they drove the Chevy into downtown Flagstaff and found a bar called Maloney's on Lenox Street. It came highly recommended by the re-stock girl in Walmart.

The place was in full swing when they arrived. Thursday was *Naughty Nurses and Dirty Docs* night: Two-for-one drinks, and waitresses costumed in nurse-white camisoles, garter belts, and stockings. A Red Cross logo was strategically placed on the front of their lacy panties, and they were serving cocktails dispensed from intravenous bags. The boys found two seats at a bar table by the window, and Matt immediately put his left hand to his chest and started crying: "Medic! Medic!"

A pretty blond dressed in the uniform of the evening – pale-skinned, red-lipped with a nurse's cap seductively pinned to the hair on the side of her head - rolled her stainless-steel stand over toward them. A large bag of translucent blue fluid hung from a hook at the top of the silver frame, and a clear plastic tube extended downward from a white valve at the bottom. A metal clip at the discharge end of the tube allowed the waitress to dispense the liquid into shot glasses kept in a circular shelf with holes, much like a communion plate.

"You're not the usual frat boys that come into my emergency room. I'll need to see some identification, gentlemen."

Matt fumbled for his wallet and produced his California driver's license. Don reached in the pocket of his fatigue jacket and pulled out his military ID. She looked them both over carefully and handed the cards back.

"My, my, my," she said, acting her part. "I just love a man in and out of a uniform!" Extending her red-polished fingernails between her tightly constricted breasts, she pulled out two thin, white mint swizzle sticks and stuck one in each of the boys' mouths. "Under the tongue, please!" she commanded. "I must take your temperature!"

She reached out and first took Matt's left hand, rotated it gently and placed two of her fingers on the inside of his wrist. Matt flicked the end of the swizzle stick with his tongue such that the exposed end oscillated rapidly up and down.

"Clever," she said, dryly. "I've never seen that before."

"Ooo," she said, back in character. "Your pulse rate is very high; you're lucky we found it out in time!" she scolded him. "I have just the thing for that!"

Compressing the clip at the end of the tube, the girl delicately filled a shot glass with blue liquid.

"Now you must drink it all at once," she admonished, "or it won't work!"

Matt threw back the shot immediately and slammed the glass down on the table.

"What is it?" Don asked.

Before Matt could answer, a short man dressed in the long white coat of a doctor - with fake bushy black eyebrows and mustache in the best tradition of Groucho Marx – inserted himself between them and into the conversation, twirling a long cigar and blinking behind his large, black-rimmed glasses.

"Mexican Viagra, boys," he smiled, arching his eyebrows up and down for effect. "But if you still have an erection after four hours, call a doctor!" Then the man turned away, hunched over and with long strides disappeared into the crowd shouting: "Doctor! Oh, Doctor!"

"Doctor, my ass," Matt laughed. "Call another nurse!"

Smiling, the girl turned her attention to Don who had remained emotionless, his eyes fixated on the girl. "I must take your blood pressure, too!" She batted her eyes and placed her fingers against the inside of his wrist while feigning a look at her watch. "We have to see if you have a pulse!"

To her surprise - based on the elevated palpitations exhibited by her previous patients that evening - this man's pulse seemed slow and probably normal by comparison. She was intrigued.

"I saw your ID, but what do your friends call you, soldier?"

"Don. What's your name?"

"Heather. You guys aren't from around here, are you?"

"Nope," Matt volunteered. "Just passing through; we'll be back on the road tomorrow, headed east."

"We need sustenance," Don said. "Is the food at this place any good?" He quickly reversed the girl's grip so that he now held her by both wrists, her palms facing upwards. "And don't lie," he added. "I'll know."

Heather laughed. *Very cute,* she thought, looking Don in the eyes for the first time, blushing as if he could read her mind.

"The food here's okay," she said, pulling her hands away to fill another shot glass. "There's a diner just down the street that's a lot better, but they don't stay open very late. You might want to get there before they close. Why don't you boys have a couple more drinks before you head out?"

She thought for a moment, then turned her head and nodded toward another faux nurse at the end of the bar. "Stephanie and I could meet you there after our shift is over."

"When's that?" Matt asked, looking across the bar toward the little brunette. He took the glass from Heather's hand and downed the second shot. "You're not sending us out for a long pass, are you?"

She ignored the question and looked at the watch on her wrist. "About a half-hour," she said to Don. "You'd better get going; once they take your order at the diner, they won't kick you out until after you've finished eating."

"Can we order you anything?" Don asked.

"Why, sure!" she answered, surprised. "Steph and I'll split a Caesar salad with chicken. They're big enough for two."

Rosie's Diner was a gleaming mass of polished aluminum, stainless steel, and glass which reflected the jeweled colors of neon lights set in parallel, horizontal lines along the top of the walls and in contrasting vertical stripes down its rounded corners, both on the outside of the structure and within. *Shiny and clean,* Don thought. As they walked up to the entrance, he saw a small sign in the window that flashed *OPEN* in brilliant green. He noticed that the white shadow of glass tubing interposed behind the current illuminated welcome also spelled out *Closed* in script, but that word had not been activated.

The men took seats opposite each other at a booth by the window. It appeared that they were the only customers in the place. The booth bench was upholstered in glowing red vinyl with a "V"-shaped panel of cream-colored material on its back. The tabletop was gray-speckled Formica with a band of pleated silver around its edge. There were vintage chrome record selectors on each table and a full-sized bubbler-type jukebox arched a rainbow of rotating colors against the wall leading to the restrooms.

Matt absently flipped the panels of the record selector at their table and noticed that the options were limited to music from the fifties. *A throwback place*, he thought.

"Doesn't work," a middle-aged woman declared from the counter. She turned to look up at the clock on the wall above the pass-through to the kitchen. "You need to order now if you want something to eat; Bob's already started cleaning the grill and the kitchen'll close in fifteen minutes."

"Yes, ma'am," Don replied. "We'd like some food. Do you have any menus?"

"Behind the jukebox your friend is playing with there," she said without looking up. "Let me know when you're ready to order."

After Matt and Don discussed their food options, Matt got up to go to the restroom leaving Don to do business with the waitress. "I'd just piss her off," Matt whispered. "You'd better deal with her."

"Ma'am," Don called to the woman. "We're ready to order now, please."

"What'll it be?" the woman barked without moving from her position, leaning on the counter to write down Don's order.

"How about two hamburgers…" he started.

"Grill's closed," she interjected without offering any alternatives.

"Okay," he replied, stalling for a few moments to look at the menu for alternatives. "Do you have any buffalo wings?"

"Bob!" she called back into the kitchen. "Is the fryer still hot?" An answer came from somewhere beyond the pass-through counter. "Yep, you want a couple of orders?"

"Yes, please," Don replied. "And could we get some fries with those wings? Do they come with salad dressing?"

"Your choice of blue cheese or ranch," she replied. "Anything else?"

"Yes," he added. "One of the large Caesar salads with chicken, please? And could we get some waters and table service for four? We're expecting two more people anytime now."

That's just swell, the woman thought. *Another couple of transients. I won't get outa here until after midnight.*

"You wanna pay for that now?" she asked, tearing off the receipt from her tablet and slapping it on the counter. "That way I can cash out for the night and get back to what I was doing."

"Sure," Don said getting up from the booth to follow the waitress to the register. He heard the pop and crackle of grease as the cook shuffled the wings and potatoes into the fryer and waited patiently while one by one the woman rang up each item on the order. He took two twenty dollar bills out of his wallet and accepted every penny of change that she offered. She looked at him with an undisguised expression of contempt on her face.

"You can leave the tip on the table," she said.

Perhaps, Don thought, *but probably not.*

As Don made his way back to the booth, Matt came out of the bathroom and slipped a dollar into the jukebox, making his first of three selections; classic rock and roll - loud and with a dominant bass beat – *sure to piss off a waitress at this time of night,* he thought.

As the music started up, the two girls from Maloney's came through the front door. The waitress felt the change in air pressure and looked up from her cash drawer and smiled.

"Well, you girls are a little early tonight! I reckon these two fellas are your dates?"

"Hi, Rosey," Heather responded, walking toward where Don was standing by the booth. "Yep – such as they are," she said smiling at him.

Heather slid into the booth wearing tight jeans stuffed into her cowboy boots, a fitted western shirt, and a slightly oversized down-filled vest. The bright red lipstick was gone, her hair fell loose and full around her shoulders, and Don was stunned. Meanwhile, Stephanie had joined Matt at the jukebox and was helping him make his last two selections, which as it turned out, were of a more mellow variety. Don continued to stand as the couple came back to the booth. Stephanie was the shorter of the two girls but was dressed like Heather. She had to use her hands to scoot across the bench, her feet not quite able to reach the floor.

"Don," Heather said, "this is my roommate Steph."

Don reached across the table to shake her hand: "Pleased to make your acquaintance," he said before sitting down beside Heather. "And this," he said, indicating his friend, "is Matt, but it looks like you two have already introduced yourselves."

"Yep, and she's already trying to change my musical tastes!"

"Shush!" Stephanie laughed. "After eight hours of hearing that in that bar, we need something a little softer, don't you agree, Heather?"

"I think Rosey would appreciate it," Heather said, just as the waitress brought over four water glasses and fussed over positioning the utensils on the napkins.

"You all just take your time," Rosey said. "Do you want anything to drink besides water?"

Matt and Don looked at each other in subdued astonishment at the change in the woman's attitude.

"The usual Diet Cokes for us," Heather said.

"That works for us, too," Matt said. "I've got to know," he added softly as the waitress moved away from their booth. "Why are we getting the royal treatment? That lady pretty much treated us like shit when we first came in."

The two girls giggled and looked toward Rosey who was putting straws in the sodas and placing them on a tray.

"We work here," offered Stephanie.

"You mean you work at the bar and here as well?" asked Don.

"Yep," answered Heather. "We work the bar from three in the afternoon until ten at night. Then we come over here to clean and lock up this place. Our night's only half over right now."

"What do you do during the day?" Don continued.

"I'm a graduate assistant at Northern Arizona University," Stephanie volunteered. "Communications department. Heather goes to school there too and works at the Administration Building," she added, leaning forward to sip on the straw of her Diet Coke while flashing a twinkling glance at Matt, who clearly looked surprised. The girls were obviously enjoying the boys' bewilderment when Rosey came over to present their food.

"There's an extra plate for you honey," she said to Heather. "And there's a few extra wings and both blue cheese and ranch dressing, too. Bob cooked up some extra fries, and I'll bring the bowl over for all of you to share in a minute. Anything else you can think of?"

"Not right now. Thank you, Rosey," Heather said, surveying the feast. "There's enough here to feed an army. Why don't you lock the door and clock out? Steph and I'll have dinner with the guys and finish up the cleaning afterwards."

"You'll be okay?"

"We'll be just fine," Stephanie answered. "Maybe with some help from these fine gentlemen we can get done early for a change," she added, punching Matt lightly in the ribs with her elbow.

Rosey locked the front door and turned the knob on the sign until it illuminated *Closed* in non-flashing red. She lowered the lights in the remainder of the restaurant and left by the back door with Bob. *Those girls have cocktailed long enough to be able to size up a guy quick,* she thought. *Clever little things.*

10

Elizabeth and Paige were standing outside the tent trailer when the boys pulled in around six the next morning. The women had gotten the family up earlier, figuring that there might be a line for the restrooms at the Walmart if they waited too long. The twins had taken Scout with them and were presumably inside the store to brush their teeth and wash their faces. Tom and Uncle Kenny were in the deli department having their thermos filled with coffee.

Why, I'd say they look rather scrubbed, Elizabeth thought, giving the boys a once-over from a distance. *I figured them to be a little hung over from whatever trouble they got into last night, but it sure doesn't look like it.*

Paige was scowling at Matt and waited until they made eye contact, before going back into the trailer. Elizabeth noticed the visual hostility that whipsawed between the two young people.

"You boys hungry?" she asked them.

"No thanks, Mom," Don replied. "We've already had breakfast. We're all set to go whenever you are."

"Why, don't you look all fresh in those new clothes. Did you have a good time last night?"

"Yes, ma'am," Matt said unashamedly, shooting a glance at Paige.

"We got to take a shower and even caught a little shuteye," Don added. "I'll tell you about it later."

"I'm intrigued!" his mother laughed. "But surely anything you'd be willing to tell me wouldn't be that exciting. Now help me get this tent folded down, please. The children should be back any minute now and the men, too. We had breakfast across the way at McDonald's, and they're all getting cleaned up in the store."

"What's the plan for today, Mom?" Don asked.

"Your father and Uncle Kenny figured that the family made such good time yesterday that we can spare a few hours to stop at the Meteor Crater Park. It's just south of our route, about an hour from here. It'll be a great surprise for the kids. I called ahead, and for a reasonable fee we can use their showers to clean up, too. We should be able to spend a couple of hours there and still get into Albuquerque by late afternoon."

"Cool," Matt exclaimed. "I've never seen a crater, have you, Don?"

"Nope, not from a meteor anyway. Just big blast holes from aerial bombs and IEDs."

"What are IEDs?"

"Improvised Explosive Devices. They used them all the time in Iraq and Afghanistan against our patrols and in suicide bombings at our bases. Deadly, but impressive, nonetheless. How big's this crater we're going to see? Do you know Mom?"

"Four thousand feet in diameter and six hundred feet deep," she replied as the children came running up. "No more talk now; it's a surprise!"

Tom and Uncle Kenny joined Matt and Don by the truck, smiling broadly.

"It wasn't what you're thinking," Don said, watching his father and uncle's expression deflate at his statement.

"But it wasn't that bad, either!" Matt whispered, winking at the two older men who immediately looked at each other and grinned, briefly remembering their own youth.

"Elizabeth, get 'em packed up and let's hit the trail," Tom called. "We're on Route 66 now, the Mother Road!"

As Tom and Uncle Kenny walked to their trucks, arms over each other's shoulders, Don heard them singing an obscure song, and he knew it was from an early black and white television show that featured two young men traveling across the country:

"If you ever plan to motor west,
Travel my way, the highway that's the best,
Get your kicks on Route 66..."

The two younger men secured Don's duffel to the bed of the truck with bungee cords then climbed into the cab.

"Are you really going to tell your folks what happened last night?" Matt asked.

"Naw," Don laughed. "My mom wouldn't believe me, and Pop would just be disappointed."

While Don's father might have been disappointed with his overnight adventure from a man's point of view, both Tom and Elizabeth would most likely have been proud of their son from a parental perspective. As the family headed out of Flagstaff and eastward into the morning sun, Don began to recall the last eight hours.

Of course, he and Matt had helped the girls mop the floors, clean the counters, and sanitize the kitchen of the diner. Matt had followed Stephanie's instruction in the front of the restaurant while Heather and Don addressed the kitchen area. All told, it had taken less than an hour. Each person worked hard to impress their partner.

"Well, that was quick," Heather said. "I need a shower, how about you guys?"

Matt perked up right away. "We have some clean clothes in the truck!"

"Are you guys staying at a hotel near here?" Stephanie asked.

"Not exactly," Don volunteered. "It would take a while to explain, but..."

"Well, then you'll have to come over to our place," Heather insisted. "But don't get any ideas; it's just for a shower."

"Where do you live?" Matt asked.

"It's not that far, and we can walk from here; that's what we normally do," Stephanie said. "But you said you have a truck?"

"Yes, ma'am!" Matt said. "It's a classic. I parked it over by the bar. We can all ride in it if you'd like."

"Why don't you and Steph take the truck," Heather suggested. "Don and I can walk. We'll meet you at the house."

"Okey dokey," Stephanie replied and without hesitating, grabbed Matt and dragged him out the back door.

Heather set the alarm on the wall, turned off the kitchen lights, and led Don out the back, pausing for a few seconds to hear the light beeping of the device assuring her that it was activated. Then she took Don by the hand, and they began their walk toward the college.

"It's just a little bungalow on the edge of campus. It's about a half hour walk to get there. I figure that's enough time for those two to accomplish what they're going to do before we arrive."

"You had that figured out, too?" Don laughed. "I thought they were going to get busy right there on the counter while we were in the kitchen."

"Stephanie's not always that easy. She broke up with one of the professors at the college about a month ago. He was married, and she got tired of spending all her holidays alone. Besides, he got his wife pregnant; I don't think he ever intended to leave her for Steph. Something about your friend really fired her up quick, though. What's his story?"

"He's been my best friend since I met him in grade school. We grew up together in San Diego. He's solid - a college graduate and a real smart guy - even though your cute little roomie has him acting about as silly as I've seen him behave in a while. He's been carrying a torch for my cousin for many years. I guess he's a little frustrated and needs some attention."

"What's your story?" she asked. "What are you guys doing out on the road?"

Heather listened intently as Don spent the next ten minutes giving a chronological version of the last eight years of his life while leaving out most of the details.

"So, I come back from Afghanistan," he concluded, "and everything is changed; my parents have been turned out of their home. My Uncle Kenny has lost a thriving business. The whole family is overnighting in Walmart parking lots across the country just to get back to an uncertain but hopeful future in Indiana."

They walked along in silence for a few minutes. There was a stone bench near the entrance to the university. "Let's sit down here for a few minutes," Heather said. The night was getting cold, so she bent her legs over Don's left thigh, put her arms around his waist and drew his body close to hers. In response, he wrapped his arms around her and leaned against the back of the bench so that she could rest her head on his chest.

"What you've told me is a little shocking, but not surprising at all," she said. "I've heard worse stories than that over the last two years, believe me."

"Really?" he asked.

"When you work at a college, you're a little insulated from the outside world, but reality is just beyond the gates. The kids that come into the bar, they seem to have no concept of the seriousness of this country's situation; they all believe that when they get out, they'll get a good job, buy a house, and be successful. The next thing you know, their parents lose their jobs and can't afford their tuition. The students take out loans that they'll never be able to repay. They end up working two, maybe three jobs to make ends meet, and they put off their future and the important things that come with it like getting married, having children."

"Is that your story, too?"

"Partially," she responded. "That's all I want to tell you for now, although I feel like I could tell you anything, and you'd understand. Do you think it's because these times appear so desperate, that human beings are drawn to one another and feel the need to reach out - even to total strangers?"

"There could be something to that," Don admitted. "But in itself, isn't that a good thing? I mean, we just met tonight but just sitting here, holding you, is the most comforting feeling that I've had in a long time."

She felt him shiver so she pulled him tighter against her body.

"Warm-blooded California puke," she laughed. "I knew it when I first saw you walk in the door."

"Oh really? So, I just wasn't a random customer? You were layin' for me, huh?"

"Uh-huh. What did you think when you first saw me?"

"It felt like someone hit me in the head with a baseball bat. I'm not talking about the nurse's outfit either, although that was – what can I say - interesting. It still feels like we've been together before, but apart for a long time."

She reached up to cradle his cheek with her hand and drew his face to her mouth. They kissed with the slow, sensuous familiarity of long-time lovers as they lingered on the bench for a while.

When Don and Heather finally arrived at the house, only the light in the kitchen was on and the door to Stephanie's bedroom was closed. Don's duffle bag was on the couch. Heather looked at him and smiled, shaking her head. "Told you," she whispered.

"Do you mind if I take my shower first? I want to sleep with you tonight, but I don't want to have sex; do you understand?"

"I would just like to hold you, too."

Heather smiled at Don and kissed him fully on the mouth. Then she tiptoed into the bathroom. After a few minutes she emerged, wrapped in a towel, her wet hair hanging in ringlets.

"I left you a dry towel on the sink," she said. "Don't be too long; I'll warm up the bed."

After taking a shower and washing his hair, Don scavenged a pair of gym shorts from the duffle and climbed into bed with Heather, who already appeared drowsy and warm.

"I set the alarm for five-thirty," she said, rolling over on her right side and wriggling her bottom against the front of his hips. "Is that all right?"

"Perfect. Good night," he whispered. Gently, he slid his left leg over her thigh, and she pressed her feet together around his ankle, pulling her body against his. Just before he fell asleep, he lightly sifted his fingers through her wet hair, spreading a few strands out over her pillow, and kissed her moist neck.

11

The old man looked out the front window of the Meteor Crater Visitor Center toward the empty road. The lower lids of his eyes were flaccid with age, and his slack jowls gave him a weary expression. His small mouth curved upward to form a counterfeit smile of welcome when Tom and Elizabeth walked in through the front door.

"Good morning!" Tom said walking up to the counter. "We called ahead to make reservations for taking showers at the campground. We're the Owens family."

"Oh, yeah," the old man said thoughtfully as he opened the cash drawer with a key on his belt. "You know, we don't usually do this. Normally, you'd have to be campin' to use the showers."

"We appreciate it very much," Elizabeth replied. "The lady I talked to on the phone said it would be alright."

"Showers are normally for campers only," the old man repeated.

"Yes, we know. We appreciate you making an exception."

"You gonna go see the crater?" the old man asked.

"Yes, please. We have four children and five adults. Do you have a family package?"

"We sure do," a middle-aged woman said as she came out of the office behind the counter. "I'm the one who talked to you on the phone, Mrs. Owens. I'm Rachel. Pleased to meet you both," she said while reaching over the counter to shake Elizabeth's hand.

"Well, we sure appreciate the opportunity to clean up," Elizabeth said.

"How long do you plan on spending with us?" Rachel asked.

"Not very long actually," Tom replied. "We've got a ways to go yet. We thought we'd let the kids visit the crater then take our showers."

"That'd be fine," Rachel said. "Just charge them a dollar each for the showers, Daddy."

The old man cast a questioning look in his daughter's direction.

"That's very kind of you," Elizabeth said. "Thank you."

"Somebody once said: *'It doesn't cost anything to look'* but that isn't always true, is it?" Rachel laughed. "If you come back by this way again, we hope you'll stay with us overnight next time."

"You bet we'll do that," Tom added. "Thank you again, ma'am."

The woman returned to her office and left the old man, humbled by his daughter's intercession, to accept the twenty-dollar bill that Tom handed him. He took the money with a palsied, shaking hand. Tom sensed a sharp pang of pity and felt like apologizing.

"The last weekend before Memorial Day," the old man stated as he gave Tom his change and tokens for the showers. "This'll be the last weekend we can take it easy until after Labor Day."

"I'll bet you get filled up real fast at the RV campground during the season," Tom replied, unable to extract himself to take his leave.

"Yep. If you'd a called the Friday before Memorial Day, we probably wouldn't have been able to accommodate you."

"Well, thanks again," Elizabeth said taking Tom by the arm and moving toward the door.

"Memorial Day," the old man repeated. "There'll be a lot of folks in, startin' Memorial Day."

"Goodbye," Elizabeth said back over her shoulder. "And thanks again."

The old man carefully shut the cash drawer and sat down on a stool near the window, fumbling with the key on his belt, waiting.

Elizabeth asked Matt and Don to escort Paige and the children down the path to the crater while she and Tom took their showers. Uncle Kenny stayed with the trucks. Paige walked ahead of the group by herself.

"Uh oh!" Don whispered to Matt. "She's pissed!"

"Let her be," Matt replied.

"There'll be a quiz on this at lunch," Elizabeth called out. "Learn something!"

The day had already started to heat up, and their clothes clung to their damp skin as Tom and Elizabeth walked back to the trucks after showering. Uncle Kenny had set up a few chairs in the lee-shadow on the west side of the Airstream.

"There's coffee in the thermos," he said. "Reckon it's my turn to get some of this road stink off. How's the water?"

"Real fine," Tom offered. "Good pressure, too."

The two of them watched Uncle Kenny, with his clean clothes rolled up in a towel, head across the parking lot toward the showers.

Tom reached down between their chairs and lifted the thermos. He removed the cup top and filled it part way with coffee, then handed it to his wife. He poured a little into a Styrofoam cup that his brother had thoughtfully inserted into the holder on the arm of his chair and held the coffee under his nose for a few moments, feeling the aroma and steam wash over his face.

"You know, Beth," he began. "I've never worried about getting old, losing my mind or my hair or having erectile dysfunction; I just don't want to become irrelevant."

"You're thinking of that old man, aren't you?" his wife said.

"Can't help it. What do you think his story is?"

"I figure that his daughter manages this place, and he's probably had to come live with her for some reason or another. She's given him that job to keep him busy, but I'd dare say that he's not too old to learn some courtesy."

"I'd say. He needs a crash course in public relations," Tom added. "If he doesn't loosen up, she won't have him up front dealing with the public for very long."

"At his age, he's probably just frustrated at having to depend on someone else for the things he used to be able to do for himself," Elizabeth said.

"It could be that or just the same old tourist-service attitude," Tom said thoughtfully, remembering their trips to Hawaii. "You know, the way workers who thrive off the tourist industry get resentful about the people who support their jobs."

"Yes," Elizabeth answered. "But there seems to be an insecurity and hopelessness that has developed in this country over the last few years, particularly among older folks; it's like they're just waiting to die instead of live. Everyone has adopted an elderly attitude; they can't see past their present situation and imagine a better future."

"You'd think that folks sharing a common burden would at least show empathy or respect," Tom said.

In the face of all this despair, Elizabeth thought to herself, *it's been a daily struggle to maintain a positive attitude. I just have to keep it together, keep the family together for a few more days, and get the family through. When we get to the farm and start to physically build our future, maybe then we'll have some direction. Right now, it's just east.*

"I think it's just plain fear," Elizabeth said, giving voice to her thoughts. "You see it everywhere. People may put on a brave act in California - the shopping malls may be filled with cars, and it might take a couple of hours to be seated at a restaurant - but they're scared."

"In the Walmart back there," Tom said. "I got the impression that the people working there acted like they were just one paycheck away from being out in the parking lot with the rest of us. They took our money, but Kenny and I noticed that they wouldn't look us in the eye."

"At least that old man showed some gumption," Elizabeth said. "Misdirected toward us, but he's clearly unhappy. He's scared and uncertain, not something any of us want to be late in life."

"You think we'll end up like that, Beth?" Tom asked. "You think that you and I are gonna have to be dependent on our kids in our old age? Sure as hell our savings are all played out, and I don't think that we can depend on Social Security or the government to live up to their promises."

"I think we'll be just fine," his wife answered. "We're a unit, you and me. We've produced some fine children, too. The way I see it, our job now is to make sure our kids maintain a curiosity and optimism for the future in the middle of all this despair. Paige must know that she's going to finish college, no matter what it takes. But we can't allow her to be saddled by student loan debt so that she will live like an indentured servant to the government for the rest of her life. Lord knows, we owe that much to Judith, rest her soul. She died way too early. I'm hoping that Don sticks around to be a role model for little Scout."

"But can we do it, Beth?" Tom asked. "What makes you think that it'll be any different in Indiana?"

"Because we've got the land, Tommy, and that's everything. We may have lost our jobs, Kenny his business, quite a few material things to be sure, but those are the *real* transient things, not us. We'll make it because we are *grounded* in the greatest sense of the word. Our children will know what it means to be stewards of their heritage. What a legacy we'll build for them! Can you imagine this happening had we not lost practically everything?"

"I'll give you that much. We pretty much lost everything."

"Except our pride, not that I think we're prideful in a religious sense. What I mean is that we still retain something inside us that makes us persevere; you and me – we don't give up!"

"Why, Elizabeth," Tom said with admiration. "You act as if we're better off now than we ever were in the last ten years!"

"Well, aren't we?" she replied. "Sometimes it takes losing everything to understand what's most important. I think we've got an opportunity to live our lives in a totally new and real way. We've been given a gift Tommy, a gift of our own making."

12

The family ended up spending more time at the Meteor Crater Park than they had anticipated. It was nearly noon before they stopped down the road for fuel. When they pulled into a rest stop an hour east of Gallup for lunch, it was already two o'clock due to the change from Pacific Daylight to Mountain Standard Time. While everyone ate, school was in session for the teenagers, and Elizabeth quizzed them on what they had learned at the Meteor Crater that morning.

"How long ago was that crater formed?" she asked. "Scout?"

"Fifty thousand years ago!"

"Julie, how big was the meteor?"

"Scientists think that it was over fifty yards across. And it struck with the impact of ten megatons of TNT!" her twin Jenny volunteered.

"That's correct Julie, but Jenny, you're answering one of my questions before I have a chance to ask it," Elizabeth laughed. "Good job, though!"

"Who can give me two modern uses for the crater besides a tourist attraction?"

Jenny raised her hand and was called upon.

"In the early 1900s, a geologist named Barringer tried to mine the iron ore from within the crater. Later, in the 1960s, I believe NASA used the crater to train the Apollo astronauts in preparation for their landing on the moon."

The quizzing went on for about half an hour. The two fathers sat back and applauded the impromptu class while Matt and Don took a walk to review the previous night in Flagstaff.

"I'll tell you what," said Matt, "that girl was a tiger! If I ever get back to Flagstaff, I'm going to look her up, that's for sure. How did your evening go?"

"By the sound of it, not as exciting as yours," Don replied. "But it did have its moments."

"Well, you did spend the night with her, didn't you?"

"Sure, but I'd rather not talk about it."

Matt sensed that he'd better drop the subject. The two friends walked in silence around the bright perimeter of the treeless rest stop.

"We can talk about it later," Don said. "Just not right now."

"Okay," Matt said. "We'll be in Albuquerque tonight. You want to go trolling again?"

"I don't know," Don replied. "Let's get there first."

The group arrived at the Walmart in Edgewood, on the eastern side of Albuquerque, just before dark. The usual flotsam of vehicles had assembled at the far corner of the parking lot - just as they had the night before in Flagstaff. The Owens children appeared more tired than expected. Elizabeth attributed it to the gradual dissipation of pent-up excitement from the beginning the adventure but also because the family had spent most of the day exposed to the drying heat and sun. *I'll have to be more careful to make sure they get enough fluid intake,* she thought, *but not before bedtime.* The Airstream had a toilet and waste storage tank, but that was for emergencies. With a parking lot full of strangers, she didn't like the idea of anyone crossing it alone to use the restroom, even though the store was open twenty-four hours.

Although everyone was road-weary and ready for bed, Elizabeth insisted that they all sit at the table for dinner. She thought it was important to establish routine and structure, even if all they had for dinner was a couple of warm pizzas that the men bought at the Walmart deli.

"Tomorrow," she announced, "we're going to have some fresh greens." Everyone groaned at the prospect.

Matt and Don participated in the pizza party and helped get the pop-up trailer ready to receive the women. Almost before they had snapped the last piece of canvas in place, the twins were inside, changing into their pajamas, snuggling halfway down the length their sleeping bags on one of the side-extended beds. Paige collected all the pizza boxes, used napkins, and soft drink cans, and disposed of them in a barrel under the light pole. She shot a sidelong glance at Matt before retiring to the safety of the trailer herself.

The adults took up positions in their folding chairs away from the glare of the storefront and watched the distant lights of the interstate traffic.

"Care to join us, boys?" Uncle Kenny asked.

"I think Matt and I are going to take a drive through the University of New Mexico," Don said. "But don't worry; we both agreed it'll just be a drive by. We won't be out too late," he added loudly so that Paige could hear. "It's already ten o'clock, and we're tired, too."

An hour after the boys left, a white sedan drove slowly through the parking lot, its headlights off. The driver switched on a spotlight by his side view mirror, flooding the canvas of the Owens' tent camper with harsh white light. Tom and Uncle Kenny rose from their seats and walked toward the car. The light swung in their direction, and they stopped mid-stride, immobilized by the beam.

"Turn that thing off!" Uncle Kenny shouted. "We can't see a damned thing!"

The driver didn't comply, for it was his intent to shake up the people camped in the lot. From behind the bright light came his disembodied voice:

"Who's in the camper?" he demanded.

"Who are you?" Tom called back.

"I said," repeated the voice. "Who's in the camper?"

"Our children," Elizabeth said loudly. "Who's asking?"

She received no response; the light stayed fixed on them. After a few moments, the Owens heard a car door open, then slam shut. Tom shielded his eyes and squinted into the bright light. He could just make out the vague shape of a man on the far side of the vehicle. The shadow squatted behind the fender, both arms extended in Tom's direction. The leaden glint of a metallic object flashed from between his clasped hands, and Tom instinctively moved in front of his wife. The night air seemed suddenly heavy and quiet, but Tom was anything but calm because he fully expected that in the next few seconds the silence would be broken by the crack of a gun. He waited for the flash, but nothing happened. Finally, the driver spoke, this time very casually.

"How long you expect to stay here?" he growled.

"Just tonight," Uncle Kenny said defiantly, not realizing that a pistol was trained on his brother. "We have permission from Walmart to be here. Who the hell do you think you are?"

"None of your business," the driver shot back. "You'd better not be here tomorrow night; you'd better move it on down the road if'n you know what's good for you!"

Uncle Kenny was preparing to move toward the voice when the tension was broken by the long blasts of their truck's horn. Paige had climbed out of the camper and crept to the truck in the shadows alongside the camper, out of the spotlight's reach. She then climbed into the cab unnoticed and was honking the horn. Headlights began to flash from all over the parking lot and other horns began to sound. Almost simultaneously, the round beams of flashlights started to bounce toward the Owens' location.

The figure on the other side of the vehicle moved quickly to get back into the car as it sped out of the parking lot and onto the adjacent frontage road. Elizabeth rushed to the cab of the pickup and opening the driver-side door, she found her niece leaning with both arms on the steering wheel, sobbing uncontrollably.

"They're gone, honey," she said, gently lifting Paige's arms from the wheel. "You can stop now; they're gone."

By the time Matt and Don arrived back at Walmart, it was after midnight. They expected to find a dark and quiet parking lot, but instead the place looked like a hive of disturbed and illuminated bees. It seemed that all the vehicles in the lot had their headlights on. As they drove the Chevy back to where the family had set up camp – away from the nearby collection of transients – they were inspected by dozens of flashlights and a few gas lanterns as the people who had responded to Paige's alarm were now dispersing and making their way back to their own trucks, trailers, and campers.

"Next time," one of the strangers said to Tom and Uncle Kenny, "park a little closer to the group. It's a little like a wagon train. Sometimes, they go after the outliers, so there's safety in numbers."

The crowd drifted back to their encampments leaving the three adults to explain to Matt and Don what had transpired. Tom said nothing about the gun. The two young men seethed with indignation and were ready to pursue the culprits, but Elizabeth counseled against it.

"They're just a couple of cowards and long gone by now."

"I'm so sorry about this," the Walmart night manager said as he hustled into the circle of light. "This is the second time this has happened in less than a month," he added. "I called the police, but they won't be out here until morning unless someone is hurt. Did anybody get hurt?"

"We're okay here," Tom offered. "But I'd like to get my hands on those assholes."

"They won't be back tonight, the bastards," Uncle Kenny added, "and we'll be out of here early in the morning anyway."

"Before you leave, stop by the office," the night manager said. "We'll set you up with some breakfast from the deli. I'm so sorry," he said again, shaking his head. "I just don't know what gets into people sometimes."

"I reckon they're just scared like everyone else," Elizabeth said.

13

Matt and Don led the caravan eastward from New Mexico toward Texas the next morning. Both young men felt like they should have been with the family the night before, and they were simmering with rage. Assuming the point position in the caravan that morning seemed to give them a freedom to discharge their anger against the road ahead instead of eddying in the turbulence at the back of the train.

"Goddammit!" Matt exclaimed. "If we'd been there those bastards would have paid for their shit!"

"Man, if we'd have got back just a few minutes earlier," Don said. "I knew we shouldn't have taken a second turn around campus. It was so quiet; there was nothing going on anyway."

"Who do you think those guys were?"

"Just some redneck locals trying to terrorize defenseless people. It's the same wherever you go. Except where I've been lately, they do it with bombs and guns."

"If this economy doesn't pick up soon, maybe next time they'll come with guns."

"The old man has one in the glove compartment of the truck. I'll bet you he has it within reach next time."

"Whoa," Matt said, looking in his rear-view mirror then at the speedometer. "You'd better slow down; you're doing seventy-five, and the family's lagging a little behind us. Besides, the old girl ain't used to flying this high."

Don had unconsciously been pressing his foot to the floorboard, and his jaw was hurting from gritting his teeth for the last hour and a half.

"Matt," he asked. "What do you say to us staying with the rest of the family from this point on? There's safety in numbers."

"I was thinking the same thing."

Elizabeth looked back over her shoulder to confirm that Scout and the twins were asleep. They had started eastward earlier than usual today, fueled by a breakfast provided from the Walmart deli by the night manager, who saw them off just before his shift ended at dawn. Tom and Kenny had taken turns sitting up the rest of the night and none of the adults had gotten much sleep.

"We were fortunate the boys weren't around last night," Elizabeth said softly to her husband.

"Why do you say that?" Tom asked.

"I think if the boys had been there, the situation would've escalated, don't you? Somebody would've gotten hurt or thrown in jail."

"You're probably right." Tom had not yet told his wife of his impression that one of the men had a gun, but he would later. He promised himself that from this day forward – regardless of where they were – his pistol would always be within reach. "Let's put that behind us. I doubt that we'll encounter anything like that again."

"Agreed," Elizabeth answered. "This family moves forward. and there's no looking back."

"I don't want you to worry too much about what happened last night, honey," Kenny said to Paige as they drove eastward. "There are some strange people in the world, and those were two of them."

"Why do you think they threatened us, Daddy? Of all people?" she sniffled. "We were just passing through."

"I think that maybe most of the folks in that parking lot have been there for a while. Didn't it look like that to you?"

"Now that you mention it, yes. Some of them looked like they had set up housekeeping."

"The way I figure it," her father said thoughtfully, "those guys last night were just scared; scared like a lot of people in towns all over the country; scared that all these people out on the road are going to end up staying in their town permanently. How would you like it if suddenly a lot of poor, desperate people descended on Ramona?"

"I think that was starting to happen before we left, Daddy," Paige answered. "They didn't congregate at a Walmart, but I'd see 'em on the way to school - down in the creek bottoms. I figured they were illegals, but the Border Patrol never did go after them; the same groups seemed to be there day after day."

Kenny shook his head, nodding first in agreement with his daughter, then side to side, as he pondered how so many lives full of hope and promise could change so radically and so quickly. He thought of his wife, Judith; Paige was so much like her mother.

"Daddy?" she asked. "We're not desperate like that are we? I mean, we're leaving California, but it's going to be better back in Indiana, isn't it?"

"By a long shot!" he answered without hesitation. "I mean it. Your Uncle Tommy, Aunt Elizabeth, and I wouldn't be putting you kids through this if we didn't think that you'd be better off in the long run. Sure, it won't be like California, but I think that we'll all thrive on the differences. You know, all the things you and I have talked about, just between us."

Paige stretched out across the seat and put her head on her father's shoulder. She had not been able to get back to sleep after the incident in the parking lot and the deficiency was catching up with her.

"Tell me about those things again, Daddy," she said drowsily. "Tell me so that I can see it."

"Well," Kenny repeated the story, just as he had since she was a little girl. "The land we're going back to was homesteaded by your great-great-great grandfather Stephen Owens in the mid eighteen-hundreds, just after the Civil War. At that time, the total holding was around six thousand acres. Can you imagine how long it took to cut trees and clear the land?"

"A long, long time."

"Over the years," Kenny continued, "bits and pieces were sold off, and by the time my grandfather, another Stephen Owens, farmed it, it was down to less than a thousand acres."

"And we bought back forty acres, right Daddy?" Paige said, then joined her father in unison:

"*Forty acres of the prettiest land in the whole state of Indiana!*" they said together.

"The soil is rich because the river comes up in the spring to fertilize the land, just as it has done for thousands of years. There's an old house on a hill above that river, so we'll just start with that. It's falling down, but we're a family of builders. We'll make it good as new with good old-fashioned hard work, and we'll live in a house that holds the spirits of our ancestors. In the spring... starting this spring, we'll plow up part of the land with a little green John Deere tractor that we'll buy with the money we've saved from California. We'll plant a big garden in order to have enough left over..."

"... to share with others that don't have as much," Paige said, prayer-like.

"That's right. And in the summer, we'll go wading in the river," Kenny continued. "And we'll seine big black schools of minnows and trap crawdads to use for bait to hook catfish as big as your arm!"

"As big as *your* arm, Daddy!" Paige yawned.

"When it's not too hot and the skeeters aren't too bad, we'll cut up the dead trees – we won't cut any down! – 'n stack it in cords to dry out so that we can split it in the fall for firewood to keep us warm. And when friends come by, we'll just say: *Why don't you have a seat by the fireplace? Can I get you a cup of tea or something to eat?* Because we'll have plenty of fruits and vegetables canned up from our own orchard and garden. We'll have a flower garden, too."

"And I'll be in charge of the flower garden," Paige said as she drifted off to sleep.

Kenny looked down and saw his late wife in his daughter – as Judith had appeared when they first met in high school. Was it really twenty years ago that she had died? He blinked back a tear then turned his attention to the road.

Kenneth Owens and Judith Shepard had met on the first day of high school when they sat by each other in Orientation Class. From that point on, they were inseparable. Two years after graduation, they married. Kenny recalled their early struggle when he worked seven days a week in the construction industry, learning how to operate heavy equipment. Strategically, Judith continued her education, attending Grossmont College at first and later transferring to San Diego State to obtain a business degree. Together they were a formidable couple, deciding to put off having children until they could build their own contracting business. This they were able to do – with Kenny's hard work in the field and Judith's management skills in the office - within ten years.

Building a business was easier than starting a family, Kenny thought. When the time finally seemed right to start that process, Judith could not get pregnant. The many doctors and specialists they visited assured them that there was nothing biologically wrong with either of them; they had merely to be patient and nature would take its course. But after concluding the decade of their thirties, it seemed clear that being parents to their own child was not to be, and both lavished their attention on Tom and Elizabeth's boy, Donovan. Then came the miracle, the decision, the joy, and the despair.

Examining her right breast one day, Judith discovered a small lump. A biopsy determined it to be a cancerous tumor, with additional involvement in the lymph nodes under her right arm. Radiation and chemical treatments were indicated but there was more. When routine blood tests were taken, they revealed that Judith was pregnant. Oncologists recommended an early term abortion so that radiation treatments could start. Judith would have none of it, even though Kenny begged her to consider the consequences.

"You got pregnant once," he had said. "You can get pregnant again."

"There's no guarantee of that," she said as they cuddled in bed. "Besides, who knows how radiation will affect our chances to conceive another child. We need to accept what the doctors said, that there's only an even chance that the treatment will save my life."

"But the doctors also said that the longer you put off treatment, the less chance you have of beating this thing. If you go full term with the baby, it might be too late for treatments to do any good."

Judith kissed the palm of his hand and gently pressed their entwined fingers against her belly.

"I will not give up this child," she said softly.

"But I can't bear the thought of losing you; I do love you so."

“Trust in God, everything will work out.”

Judith’s pregnancy was terminated at eight months with the premature delivery of her daughter Paige by Caesarian section. Within days of the birth, Judith was started on a regimen of treatment for the disease. But as foreseen by her oncologist, the chemicals and radiation chased the disease but could not catch it. She died in the third month following parturition from her child. After the mourners had left the little cemetery above the Flat Rock River, Kenny knelt beside her grave and made two promises: that their daughter would never be burdened with the knowledge of her mother’s sacrifice and that he never again would trust in God.

“We’ll plant some of your mother’s favorites: tulips, daffodils, and especially irises,” he said softly, stroking his daughter’s hair. “We’ll cut some flowers every Sunday to put on her grave in the little cemetery just down the road. She’ll be looking down on us from heaven. And there’ll be all the showy annuals… just exploding in whites, yellows, red, blues, and pinks. We’ll cut them and hang them upside down on the back porch so that they dry out and their colors will never die.”

Oh, Judith, he thought. *We’re coming home.*

14

"Why do they call them picnic areas? Who would want to stop there?" Matt complained, pointing to a strip of asphalt beside the highway lined with a series of four, thinly corrugated roofs set on metal poles about twenty feet apart, each providing shade to an overflowing trash barrel. "There're no restrooms, no water, no shade - not even anywhere to sit. It's like the State of Texas just wants you to keep moving on."

"I don't think there was one public restroom between Tucumcari and Amarillo," Don responded, taking his turn at the wheel of the truck. "It doesn't look like there'll be one between Amarillo and Oklahoma either. How long until we get to Elk City?"

"We just passed Shamrock, Texas," Matt said while flipping the pages of the road atlas. "I'd say we'll be there in less than an hour, way before dark. The Walmart is on old Route 66, so look for that exit."

"Once we get settled, we should walk into town and check out some of the old buildings along the highway," Don suggested. "We haven't really done that yet. I got a glimpse of a few old hotels and burger places when we stopped in Santa Rosa."

"They all appeared to be closed," Matt mused. "Can you imagine the impact that this interstate had on all those businesses when it was built? Look at all the little towns we've gone around so far that Route 66 used to pass through. I wonder what happened to the people that ran those shops?"

"Well, some of the little hotels appeared to still be open, but I'll bet they can't compete with the larger chains. I saw some of the neon signs that advertised *Free Cable TV* or *Pool*; but you know, that's just standard stuff anymore at the bigger hotels. Hell, they even have free breakfasts, and you know that appeals to most families with kids."

"But what do you think happened to all those people who were run out of business and displaced?"

"I dunno," Don answered. "I've always had the impression that most of those small businesses were started by guys that came back from World War II. You know what I mean? Greasy spoon kinda truck stops or service stations where they pumped your gas, washed your windows, and checked your oil; places where they fried real hamburgers from fresh ground beef, instead of frozen cow parts; garages where the mechanic could diagnose and repair your car without hooking it up to a computer. I'd imagine that after the interstate went in those guys held on for a while. After you've survived a war, you probably get the impression that everything else has got to be a lot easier. Eventually they lost their businesses, not just to the interstate, but to the uniformity of the fast food and hotel chains. I imagine that they took the same road that put them out of business to a new life somewhere else."

"I heard once that the business model that Ray Kroc developed – he's the guy that started MacDonald's - was that families traveling across country would want consistency in the type of food they could get," Matt said. "Evidently, he was right."

"I guess that same principle applies to just about everything from MacDonald's to Holiday Inns to Walmarts. You know what you're getting going in. Not a lot of variation unless you get off the beaten path. Hell, in most of the major cities I passed through in the Middle East, Asia, and Europe, they've got a Kentucky Fried Chicken and right next to it, a Taco Bell and a Pizza Hut."

"Comin' up on Elk City, Oklahoma," Matt announced as they began a long sweeping turn to the north. "I think the Walmart's at the next exit."

Don steered the truck off Interstate 40, and the rest of the caravan followed him onto a section of Route 66 that ran through the middle of Elk City. Don saw the familiar blue sign as they approached the parking lot. Both sides of the road were lined with people holding up signs that read: *Stop Walmart! Walmart Out of Elk City!* and other messages along the same line. Don slowed the truck to make the turn across the divided highway into the parking lot. At the vegetated median a swarm of people gathered around the lead vehicle. The crowd appeared to be composed of average people: middle-aged men and women with a few children hovering in the open areas behind them. They didn't appear disorderly or bent on any violence.

"They look like a friendly-enough lot," Matt said. "Don't hit anybody or you'll just piss 'em off."

A heavy-set man in a worn Stetson hat approached the driver's side of the truck. Don rolled down the old Chevy's window and casually leaned an elbow out.

"What's going on here?" he asked.

"You goin' shoppin' at the Walmart?" the Stetson man asked.

"We planned to spend the night in the parking lot," Don answered. "Us and the two trucks behind us. We're moving across country to Indiana."

"Well, we can't stop you from doin' that, but we'd be grateful if you'd not buy anything at the store."

"It seems to me it's a free country and a man ought to be able to come and go as he pleases," Don answered.

The man put his big hand on the rain gutter of the door and leaned in toward Don. His manner remained casual and neither Don nor Matt perceived a threat.

"Look, all these people are folks that own businesses in Elk City, just the other side of the interstate there. Walmart's applied to build a new Super Store on the west side of town and abandon this one. That means that any business in town that's not already been affected so far is gonna take a hit, probably be put outa business. We've seen it all over this state before. Entire centers of little towns goin' bankrupt. There's a term for it you know. We call 'em *Walmart Deserts.*"

"He's right," Matt said to Don. "I've seen it happen even in the larger cities like San Diego."

"If you're interested," the man continued, "there's a gatherin' at the park across from the post office in town tonight if you'd care to join us."

"How do we get there?" Matt asked.

"Just go down this street until you get to the center of town. The post office is off to your right. Don't worry, there'll be a lot of people showin' up; you'll find your way."

Before any other words could be exchanged, the whoop of a siren punctuated the air as a police cruiser – its lights flashing blue, white, and red - pulled slowly up beside the Chevy. The crowd parted and resumed their stations at the side of the road. An Oklahoma State Trooper got out of the car, adjusted the leather band on the back of his Smoky-the-Bear hat, flipped up his clip-on sunglasses, and approached Don's side of the truck.

"You can't stop here. What's your name?" he demanded.

"Owens," Don replied. "Don Owens. And that's my family behind me," he added, jerking his thumb at the vehicles that had pulled up close behind him.

The trooper turned his head slowly to the two following trucks and took out a pad of paper from his shirt pocket. He walked to the back of the line of vehicles and started writing down license plate numbers as he walked to the front of the family line.

"You plan on stopping here for the night?" he asked.

"Just for the night," Don answered. "We're just passing through on our way east."

"Okay, then," the trooper said. "Just pull through the lot to the south side and get in line with everyone else. I'd advise you not to mix with this crowd. Just go about your business and be gone in the morning. If I catch you here more than one night, I'll run you in."

Don was tempted to demand: *Run us in for what?* But instead, he swallowed his anger and answered: "Yes, sir," and pulled into the parking lot followed by the rest of the family caravan. They were directed to a long line of vehicles queued up along the perimeter of the expansive parking area.

"Damn, this is gonna take a while," Don said. "And it feels like it's getting hotter. You figure there's a storm coming?"

"If not a rainstorm, then a shit storm," Matt replied.

"There's something really wrong going on here. All those people along the road gave me the willies. That state trooper looked at us like we were trash, and now we're being inspected by those rent-a-cops up ahead."

"Aw, those folks on the road seemed pretty average to me. Maybe a little desperate. Even that trooper seemed okay – a little resigned to doing a job he didn't like; he didn't give any of those protesters any shit."

"He probably lives in town and knows most of 'em,"

"You've not been back that long, Don," Matt said, as they waited in line. "What you're seeing is a lot of dissatisfaction and desperation that's been growing in the country for the last few years. It's happened to us out in California - those assholes that accosted your folks in the parking lot last night - the protesters along the road when we came in - people going against each other, trying to hold onto what they have. I'm surprised there haven't been riots in the streets and people marching on the government like scenes from the French Revolution; pitchforks, axe handles and shit like that. I don't think it's going to get much better in the short term."

"But do you think Mom, Dad, and Uncle Kenny are pulling the family into a bad situation back in Indiana? If it's getting worse, like you say, what can we expect there?"

"What they're doing may seem quite sudden and impulsive to you, but they've had some time to consider all their options. Your folks wouldn't just pack it up and leave if they didn't think it would be better than California," Matt replied. "For better or for worse, your family has a place to live, a house to improve, and land to work. So, no matter what else gets thrown at them they have each other and a place to live."

"But in general, you're pretty pessimistic about the state of the country, huh?" Don asked.

"Pretty much," Matt replied. "You'll see what I'm talking about in time. I'm just saying that there's something that's been going on in this country that's creating a lot of unease and friction. There'll be a blow-up; it's just a question of where and when. It's like high and low fronts coming together to create a thunderstorm." And with this last statement Matt quit speaking and looked out the window to the south at the tops of cumulus clouds absorbing the last orange rays of the sunset.

"Name," the security guard demanded as he walked up to the driver's side of the truck.

"Owens," Don replied. "Still Don Owens, and those two trucks behind us are Owens, too."

"Number one fifty-seven," the guard said to his partner as he handed Don an orange post-it with the number broadly hand-printed by a felt marking pen. The guard's partner wrote down the figure on a clipboard alongside their license plate number.

"Put this in your windshield. Park over there. Next!" he called out, pointing Don toward an empty area of the lot and motioning for the next vehicle in line to pull up.

"This is just too weird," Matt said.

Humiliating, Don thought. *It's like a scene from the Grapes of Wrath.*

15

The family set up their camp in the northeast corner of the parking lot near a small clump of trees. Elizabeth, as she had promised, created a large salad of three types of lettuce, avocados, tomato wedges, carrots, and mushrooms. In deference to the men of the group, she added slices of chicken, ham, and cheese. Two big Tupperware bowls were prepared in this way and set out on one of the collapsible tables along with two gallons of green tea, all purchased at Walmart.

After dinner the adults, including Paige, lounged in the director's chairs while the children huddled in the camper trailer, competing on a portable video game. The night air was heavy with moisture and the occasional breeze brought no relief from the heat. In consequence, no one thought to add the warmth generated from the gas lantern to the evening; the cool, blue mercury-vapor lights suspended from poles high above the lot seemed to suffice. Compared to the other stores they had stopped at along the way, there were noticeably fewer transients in this lot.

"You reckon they were intimidated by the crowds?" Tom asked Kenny.

"No doubt," his brother answered. "If Don hadn't pulled on through, I would have just gone on to the next town."

"That would've been Oklahoma City," Elizabeth offered. "And that's too far. We would've gotten in after dark, and the kids were pretty much done for the day."

"Boy, the air is close tonight," Tom offered. "I guess we'll keep the windows rolled down in the truck. There's hardly a breeze. Are you girls gonna be okay in the trailer?"

"We'll be just fine," his wife answered. "I want to get out of here early in the morning before those protesters come back. I don't have a good feeling about this place."

Don and Matt had lowered the tailgate of the truck and were sitting on it apart from the other members of the group. Their hands gripped the edge of the warm metal. Their legs, bent at the knees, swung below them like schoolchildren too small for their desks.

"It looks relatively safe here," Matt offered. "I think we ought to go into town."

"Really?" Don asked. "After all that, you still want to go along Route 66?"

"No," Matt replied. "I want to go to that meeting in the town park. I wanna hear those speakers that man talked about. You think your folks would mind?"

Don considered his friend's suggestion for a few minutes.

"I know what my dad would say," he finally answered. "Pop would say that it ain't no business of ours. Mom would say that there's no good that can come of it, that we'd better just look after ourselves and move on."

"Maybe so," Matt said. "But it seems to me that there's something going on in this country that meeting is the product of; I mean, in a way I think that meeting is real democracy in action. I wanna see it."

"What do you mean, *democracy in action*?" Don asked.

"Think about it for just a minute," Matt answered. "I've had the last three months hiding out in the old neighborhood to think about it myself."

"Go ahead, I'm listening."

Matt began:

"I figure that the local government decided it was okay to put a Walmart here in Elk City, just like planning and zoning commissions make the decisions about where to place schools, housing developments, and everything else in a community. You know that's true because your family's in the construction business."

"I'd say that you're right about that."

"Then why, if the people of Elk City didn't want a Walmart, why did they let the planning and zoning people approve it in the first place; why don't they have any control over its expansion?"

"What are you getting at?"

"I think that everyone in town, especially the people in charge, liked the idea of a Walmart in the beginning and approved of the store without thinking of the consequences. It's because they figured the town stood to benefit from the cheap prices, maybe employment, and all that. I'll bet you Walmart made a pretty good case, too. After a while, when people started seeing local businesses collapse, they got scared, and now they're against an expansion."

"So why don't they take it up with the planning and zoning folks in town?"

"I figure that it must be too late for that, otherwise, why would they be protesting out on the highway and gathering at a meeting in town? I'll bet you the expansion's already been approved, and there's nothing that can be done about it."

"So why do you think that this meeting is democracy in action?"

"Because this little, local form of government represented by the planning and zoning people is not listening to the people from its community. It's largely unresponsive to its citizens, only responsive to the big business of Walmart. Those folks out on the highway today and at the park tonight are disenfranchised; they think that they have no say in the matter anymore. They're gathering tonight to explore some alternatives, and I'll bet you – remember that old man said that there'd be some speakers from outside the community – that some of those alternatives may not be exactly peaceful."

"Are you kidding me? Are you saying that those folks will attack the Walmart? You've got to be joking."

"Maybe not this Walmart. But this ain't the only place in the country where people are feeling left out. I'll bet there are a thousand Elk City, Oklahomas all over the country and millions of people who feel that their futures are in jeopardy, that the government isn't listening to them. One small town in Oklahoma railing against a big corporation is one thing but two hundred... three hundred towns? That's a movement! Look at our own situation. The government steps in to help Wall Street and the banks because they were too big to fail. Yet the citizens that elected that government, and their children and grandchildren, are going to be saddled with that debt, even as they lose their jobs and their homes. Do you think that anyone in Washington asked the common man whether they wanted a bailout?"

"They have elected folks in Washington that are supposed to represent them, don't they?" Don said.

"You just made my point," Matt laughed. "Don't you see, Don? There's a growing sense that no one's looking out for the common citizen, that government is no longer representative of the people and for the people. Well, that meeting tonight *is* democracy in action because I figure that the folks in Elk City are going to get what they want one way or another."

16

It was nearly nine o'clock when Matt and Don headed from the family camping area to the Walmart entrance. As they drove up to the West 3rd Street exit – as Route 66 is called when it passes through Elk City - two men stood up from chairs positioned on either side of the entrance. Swinging low arcs with their red lanterns, they indicated for the truck to stop. A bobbing flashlight approached Matt on the driver's side, and the shadowy figure behind it shone a bright beam directly in Matt's face, then swung it over to illuminate Don.

"Where do you think you're going?" the shadow-man demanded.

"Just into town," Matt answered. "There a law against that?"

"Don't get smart with me, buddy!" the man responded.

"What do you mean?" Don said. "We're camped down at the end with our family!"

"Oh, yeah? What's yer name?"

"Owens… Don Owens."

The security guard repeated Don's name to the other guard at the front of the truck. After a few moments, Matt heard the guard say: "Yep, he's on the list."

"Sure, go on into town," the man with the flashlight said, "but don't come back here afterwards."

"What do you mean?" Matt asked.

"I said, if you leave, yer gone," the man said coldly. "This exit is one-way tonight."

Matt exchanged a quick glance toward Don who was shaking his head, his jaw tight with indignation. Without saying another word, Matt shifted into reverse, backed into the parking lot, and drove to where the family was camped in the shadow under the clump of trees. He turned off the truck's ignition and lights and the engine rumbled to a stop. After a few moments, he spoke to Don.

"Now what do you want to do?" he said. "Sonofabitch!"

"I sure as hell am getting tired of being pushed around," Don responded. "This is bullshit!"

"Yeah, who in the hell do they think they are? Jeez, this is just as bad as those assholes driving into the lot last night to intimidate your folks. The only difference is that these assholes had badges."

"Let's go see what's going on," Don said, opening his door. "We don't need no stinking badges!"

They quickly moved under the darkness toward the northern embankment at the edge of the parking lot. Before they could scale the tall chain-link fence, they threw themselves to the ground as a night watchman passed by on the other side of the enclosure. Don motioned for Matt to wait for a few moments until the guard disappeared behind a corner of the stockade. Then - as if in one motion - they silently clambered over the top of the barrier and dropped to the other side, half running, half-rolling down into a ditch.

They jogged across a long grassy field in the darkness until they came to an asphalt road running north to south. They crossed the road and another open field until they came to a baseball diamond that was lit up with adults playing slow-pitch softball. Staying away from the crowds that appeared intent on watching the game, the two friends turned south and continued down a darkened street until they rejoined Route 66.

"Hold up for a minute!" Matt cried out. "I gotta get my breath. I haven't been chasing terrorists for the last six months like you."

Matt bent over, hands on his knees and tried to draw in the cool night air. Don waited patiently beside him and looked up the long boulevard. In the distance, there appeared to be a line of slow traffic headed east up the street and a stream of pedestrians moving across it at each intersection where there was a stoplight.

"You've gotten soft," Don said with a chuckle. "A few months outta work and you've become a real pussy! Like the man said, we won't have any problem finding the meeting: look at all those people on the move!"

Matt stood upright and gazed at the sign for the Route 66 Museum. He put his hands on his hips, and his words came less labored as he appeared to have caught his breath.

"I'll bet this town hasn't seen this much late-night activity for years!"

"I dunno. It's like everyone's cruising Route 66."

"Let's go," Matt said excitedly. "I don't want to miss anything!" and he started running down the street toward the crowd.

Don too felt a magnetism in the air and jogged off after his friend. In the distance, they could hear muffled applause punctuated now and then by a few honking horns.

Floodlights had been set in the open area of the park illuminating a small panel of people seated on risers. In front of them was a podium that had been borrowed from the library down the street. By the time the boys arrived, there seemed to be around a hundred people in attendance, and it appeared that the meeting had been going on for some time. It was distinctively a well-dressed older crowd – clothed as if for a religious revival – and most of the people had brought along folding chairs. The current speaker was the man in a Stetson hat who appeared to be the evening's emcee.

"So, how about that?" he asked, and the crowd responded with polite applause. From the back came an unintelligible but a clearly derogatory shout. The older people up front turned around, and someone shouted again, a horn was honked, and a car sped away.

"Our next speaker is Norma Fines," the speaker said, ignoring the outburst and calling the crowd's attention back to the podium. "Some of you may know her; shoot, most of us took her civics class in high school. Miss Fines?" he said, indicating for a frail, elderly woman to approach the podium. The man pushed down the flexible microphone stand to a lower height to accommodate the smaller speaker who was almost invisible behind the podium.

"Testing, testing," Miss Fines spoke into the microphone, tapping its foam-covered head a few times for reassurance. The tinny speakers squealed slightly with feedback as someone adjusted the volume.

"Charlie? Is that okay?" she asked. "Then let's get started." The tiny woman took a deep breath and practically shouted into the microphone.

"The right of workers to organize labor unions is a basic human right!" she cried, and the crowd responded with stunned silence. Miss Fines then adjusted her spectacles and read slowly and deliberately from her notes, emphasizing specific words within the quotation:

"In 1935 Congress enacted the National Labor Relations Act, and I quote: '*to protect the rights of employers and employees, to encourage collective bargaining, and to curtail certain private sector labor and management practices which can harm the general welfare of workers, businesses, and the United States... economy!'"* At the end of her declaration, she pointed a thin index finger into the air and shook it for emphasis.

A middle-aged man standing to one side of the crowd began to giggle rather loudly. Miss Fines looked in his direction over the top of her spectacles.

"You'd know that, Lester Stewart!" she said. "If you'd a been payin' attention in class instead of playing footsie with Sally Barnes in the back row!"

A shriek came from somewhere far back in the darkness, and the crowd rumbled with laughter. Miss Fines shook her head from side-to-side, waited for the cackling to settle down then continued.

"Now, this state doesn't pay teachers the best, my State Pension, Social Security, and Medicare only go so far. So, like a lot of folks, I needed a little extra income. I started to work for Walmart in nineteen and ninety-nine, right after I retired from teachin' y'all for forty-six years! The Walmart started me out at eight dollars and twenty-five cents an hour 'n twenty-eight hours a week. I can get by on that. But what about the younger folks here in Elk City?" she cried. "Those wages are below the poverty line. The manager at Walmart only lets 'em be paid for twenty-eight hours a week; I say *paid* because he forces us to work off the clock... through our breaks... and even deletes any hours over twenty-eight from our time sheets without askin'. That's because if you work under twenty-eight hours you're not entitled to any benefits! It ain't right!"

The crowd reverberated, and Miss Fines waited for silence. *These proceedings are beginning to take on the feel of a revival meeting,* Don thought as he looked toward Matt, who was smiling.

"In the long run," the teacher said, "the employees make so little that most are below the poverty level and qualify for government aid. Why, just last year a study showed that Walmart employees in the State of California received over twenty billion dollars, *twenty billion dollars* in health care assistance from the government! And who do you think pays for that? Lookie here, I found this report by the House Committee on Education and Welfare. It says that a two hundred-person Walmart store – like the one we got here in Elk City - costs taxpayers around four hundred thousand dollars a year; that's over two thousand dollars per employee." She paused for emphasis. "And who do you think pays for that?"

"We do!" several people cried out in unison.

"Now, I'm an old lady and a serious threat to Homeland Security, I guess," she said, and the crowd responded to her self-deprecating humor. "Because las' week, I got fired from my Walmart job for speakin' up at a meeting about such things. Now, I don't have no great love of unions, but my momma always said: *'Find a need and fill it!'* So, I spoke up and said that if we had a union, we wouldn't be required to work a lot of our hours for free, and we'd have benefits to boot! Well, that went over like a lead balloon. After the meeting was over, they escorted me to the front door; they had already clocked me out!"

The former teacher had finished lecturing on what she wanted to convey to the crowd, so she turned to face the speakers sitting behind her and smiled. In turn, her former students applauded their appreciation along with the crowd. The man in the Stetson hat helped the woman back to her seat. He then returned to the podium and lifted the microphone, stretching out the flexible stand to its original position.

"Okay, folks," he began. "I want to thank all the previous speakers for their insight into various aspects of our common problem. We've heard from the bank; we've heard from the Chamber of Commerce; we've heard from the Mayor on how the town's been affected by the current Walmart; Miss Fines just gave us some insight into what it's like to work at Walmart. So, let me summarize tonight's entertainment." He paused for a few moments, lifted his hat with one hand and swept a handkerchief across his brow with the other, then began to speak, slowly increasing the speed of his words.

"It seems we all agree that the lives of the people of Elk City - inside and outside the store – have been changed one way or another since Walmart came to town. Mister Lester says that all the money that's deposited in his bank from Walmart is wired out of town to Bentonville, Arkansas within hours and doesn't add anything to the local economy. He says people working at the Walmart don't even bank with him anymore; they cash their checks on Friday at the store when they get their groceries and pay cash for everything else that food stamps and welfare won't cover. Mister Elmore at the Chamber of Commerce explained to us the value of shopping locally - that if you spend ten dollars at Johnnie's Food Basket, Johnnie will take some of that money to buy some flowers for his wife, Jenny, at Edna's, and Edna might take some of that money to buy a new dress at Gert's and so on and so forth. Those ten dollars stay in the community to support our businesses, our schools, our town – each other, really."

There was a scattering of applause and many of the crowd nodded in agreement.

"The mayor told you how much more it's gonna cost the town to lay in new water lines and sewers, widen the roads, and run power out to the new store. What he failed to mention is that once the new store is built, the other will lay fallow until Walmart sells it; but they ain't gonna sell it to their competition and Lord knows, only another large retailer will buy that place!"

From the back of the assembly came some muffled shouts and movement outside of the glare of the floodlights.

"And Miss Fines," the speaker continued nervously, sweeping his hand toward where his former teacher sat in the row behind the podium. "Miss Fines gave us a pretty good picture of what it's like to work at the Walmart. She was able to do this because they fired her last week. Anyone else that works there was afraid to speak tonight because they'd lose their job!"

The sounds from the back of the crowd grew noticeably stronger. The man again removed his hat and wiped his brow. He gripped both sides of the podium with his big hands and leaned forward, turning his head from side to side, gathering in the people with his silence. His voice took on a deeper, almost spiritual tone reserved for preachers when they get to the part in their sermons calling down hellfire and damnation.

"So, what do we do?" he at first asked plaintively. "Do we just sit around and take it?"

"No!" a few people shouted.

"We can't stop the new store because the Town's already approved it. So, what's keeping us from marching across the road and burning down the old Walmart?"

The crowd was stunned to silence. Don looked at Matt. Both young men's eyes were wide with shock.

"Oh my God," Don whispered. "You don't think they're serious, do you?"

"Hold on for a minute," Matt muttered. "I think he's about to make his point."

"No, we're not going to do that," the man said, shaking his head in resignation. "And you know why? Because we're decent folks, and we don't do things like that and because," he paused a moment for effect. "Because *we* are part of the problem – and we have it within our power to be the solution!"

The commotion at the back of the gathering got louder. A few of the people seated at the front stood up and, shielding their eyes from the floodlight, they craned their necks toward the darkness behind them. A person separated himself from the obscure mass in the back and ran down the street, followed a few seconds by a small group of shadows.

"Please, please!" the speaker shouted. "Please!" After a few moments the crowd settled down and returned its attention to the podium.

"Do you realize," he continued, "that by shopping at the Walmart we keep our families and friends in a perpetual state of poverty? That by shopping at Walmart we are paying higher prices when you consider all the public assistance we provide to the corporation and their workers? By shopping at Walmart, we're supporting sweatshops and child labor in third world countries!"

He spoke more softly now so that the crowd would automatically strain to hear his words. "There's a real simple solution to Walmart," he said. "We've got to quit patronizing them; each of us has got to quit shopping there – not just one of us - all of us! We've got to put the needs of the many ahead of our own self-indulgence."

Matt watched the reaction of the crowd. *Keep it local,* he thought to himself. *Don't talk about sweat shops, global warming, or anything remotely related to a universal truth. These people aren't going to be interested in that. They're interested only in themselves – low prices and convenience. They sure aren't going to let someone tell them what to do even if they'll benefit in the long run.* "I don't think they're getting it," he whispered to Don.

"I got a right to shop where I want!" someone cried from the back.

"Communist bastard!" someone else yelled. "Red!"

"Don't you see the connection?" the speaker implored. "We all shop at the Walmart because the prices are low, but those prices come at a cost. How do you think they keep prices down to attract our business? By beating down the people that supply the products, especially those that are made in America; by buying from overseas manufacturers where people are paid eight dollars a day – not eight dollars an hour - to make clothes or toys; by getting tax breaks and infrastructure like roads and utilities paid for by the town; and yes, by paying lower wages to our neighbors, making them rely on public assistance to make up the difference in their take home pay and benefits. If we all just paid a few cents more for a shirt or blouse to keep Americans employed in American businesses…"

A wedge seemed to have been driven down the middle of the park as people began leaving left and right of the podium. The exodus started to gain momentum as if someone had detected the first drops of an approaching rainstorm. In response, the speaker attempted to adopt a less provocative tone and called out to the crowd, trying to appease his departing neighbors.

"The Walmart store isn't evil - the people working there are decent folks like you and me just trying to provide for their families, but they can't even do that on what they're paid. We need to take back our town by supporting our home-grown businesses and people; that's all I'm saying!"

The retreat became general until only a few people remained at the front and even so, they were alerted to what seemed to sound like an organized opposition that came from the rear. As people left the gathering, they were jeered and harangued by a large group of thugs, young men who seemed less interested in standing up for Walmart but more bent on anarchy. The sound of distant sirens could be heard, and the flashing lights from squad cars could be seen speeding down the highway from the west. Without warning, the microphone was silenced, and the flood lights went out.

"We need to get out of here quick," Don said to Matt. "This thing's going to escalate before the police get here."

Matt hesitated for a moment. "What about these old people?"

"I don't think those goons will mess with the folks that are sitting down," Don replied. "They have all they can handle with the ones that are walking away. The police will be here before that happens. C'mon!"

17

Matt followed Don as he rushed past the speakers' platform and disappeared into the darkness behind the podium. As they jogged west on 5th Street they saw three police cruisers flash by a few blocks up on 3rd Street, heading east to the park. Distant sirens could be heard approaching from the opposite direction, coming in from the interstate to the south. When 5th Street ended at Brian Road, they sat in the shadows under a large tree for fifteen minutes before Don got up and headed north to Highway 40. Matt followed his friend. When they reached Broadway they slowed to a walk and turned left. A few blocks down, they saw the lights of a tavern and a vehicle-crowded parking lot.

"Hang on a minute," Matt said, moving into the darkness outside the cone of light from a streetlamp. "Don't you think it's awful strange that so many police responded to this thing – and so quickly?"

"What are you getting at?"

"I wouldn't have thought there were that many police on duty in this town, and I think that some of those cruisers were state police."

"Yeah. They aren't just generally sitting around out on the interstate ready to respond to domestic violence, especially around here. Who do you think those troublemakers were?"

"I'll bet you that they're a bunch of angry, unemployed guys just looking to start something," Matt said. "I'll bet you it didn't have a lot to do with Walmart at all."

"You think they just took advantage of a gathering, huh?"

"It's a Saturday night, you're unemployed; you've got no money to take a girl out or do anything. I suppose it'd be pretty frustrating."

"I got a little bit of a glimpse of them," Don said as they began to walk toward Knucklehead Red's Saloon. "They looked like a bunch of skinheads to me."

"Wait a second, buddy," Matt said, taking the measure of the bar toward which they were walking. "Those sonsabitches probably scattered when the cops arrived. It's probably not a good idea to go past that bar up ahead. You never know who might come out."

"Good idea," Don replied. The two of them cut north through some hotel parking lots and crossed the highway near where they had come out from the Walmart a few hours before. When they reached the edge of Ackley Park, the softball diamonds were mostly dark except for one feeble security lamp near the concession stand that cast its inadequate, anemic light over the fields. They walked north up a grassy path hemmed in on both sides by low fences that separated the ball fields. As they neared one of the diamonds, Matt saw two figures emerge from the shadows of a dugout. He tapped Don on the arm and pointed them out to his friend.

"One of them has a bat," Matt said, "and I don't think he's interested in playing ball."

The two figures stopped a short distance in front of where Don and Matt were walking, barring their way. The person with the bat held the weapon lazily over his shoulder and rotated it with his right hand. Both boys were short, skinny and with their heads shaved, appeared to be only high school age or a little older.

"You wanna fight?" the batter asked, his eyes quickly glancing first from Don then back to Matt, who almost laughed at the prospect.

"Not on our list of things to do tonight," Don answered, moving closer, almost shoulder-to-shoulder with his friend.

"Well," said the other boy. "We wanna fight you!"

"Ain't gonna happen, gentlemen," Matt said. "Go home now; its way past your bedtime."

"We don't have to take no shit from you!" the one with the bat spat back at Matt, tucking his chin into his chest, trying to make his whiny voice sound bolder and impressive.

Damn, Don thought, *what we have here are a couple of room-temperature IQs out to impress someone.* He heard a horn honk behind them. Looking back over his shoulder he saw a dozen or more men clustered on the other side of the highway preparing to cross to the park while a few others had already dodged traffic and were moving hurriedly to the confrontation.

"You don't want to mess with us," he heard Matt say. "This here's a U.S. Special Forces Marine, lately arrived from kicking raghead ass in Afghanistan – and I ain't no slouch – so back off!"

Much to his surprise, the two boys held their ground, and Matt was caught off guard when the one to his left raised his bat into the air and rushed at Don who was looking over his shoulder toward the highway.

"Lookout," Matt cried as the boy swung his bat at Don's head.

It was just enough warning. Don ducked in time to avoid the blow, but Matt, standing close to his friend, took the full force of the tapered metal cylinder against his left shoulder. Matt dropped to his knees, momentarily stunned, and watched – in a dream-like state – as Don in one slow and continuous motion, wrenched the bat from the teenager's clenched hands, planted his boot into the ribs under the boy's extended right arm as he turned to face their other attacker. Don slammed the bat into the side of that boy's knee, cracking it inward as the youngster yelped in pain and fell to the ground.

As Matt struggled to his feet, his right hand clasping his left arm, Don walked over to the first boy who was lying prostrate on the ground. He grasped the boy's right wrist and pulled him to one side of the partitioned path to gain a defensive perimeter. He placed his boot on the boy's neck and pulled on his arm until the youngster cried out in pain. He brandished the baseball bat at the group advancing from the highway.

"C'mon, you bastards!" he called out. "Who wants it next?"

Matt turned to see a line of men approaching from a few yards away. He reached down and grabbed the second boy by his jacket collar then dragged him screaming toward Don. Matt threw the crying boy up against the chain link fence and took up a position next to his friend.

One of the men in the dark troop snapped his finger and the confederacy formed a half-circle around Don and Matt, the ends of which intersected the fence on either side of where the duo stood and waited. After a brief standoff, a large man in the middle of the arc –

bluish tattoos on his neck and bare arms that were visible in the dim light – moved challengingly forward and addressed himself to Don.

"There's more a' us than there is a' you," he growled. "We're gonna kick your Commie asses so ya might as well let those boys go now!"

"I don't think so," Don replied. "I figure to break this one's neck to start off with, and we'll get a few knocks in before we go down, starting with you!"

The man smiled grimly and looked at the two cringing boys on the ground.

"We don't much give a shit about those two. *God choseth the weak things of the world to shame the strong,"* he said, adding, "First Corinthians, chapter one, verse twenty-five."

Don replied, "*He chose the lowly things of this world and the despised things - and the things that are not - to nullify the things that are, so that no one may boast before him. Therefore, as it is written: Let him who boasts, boast in the Lord."* First Corinthians, Chapter One, Verses twenty-seven through twenty-nine."

The big man's eyes widened then narrowed. His grin turned downward as he glared toward Don. Then he raised his arms into the air and in a beseeching voice cried, "*O Lord of Heaven's Armies! You test those who are righteous, and you examine their deepest thoughts and secrets. Let me seek your vengeance against them, for I have committed my cause to you!"* Jeremiah Twenty, Verse twelve," he added.

The man seemed very pleased with himself and sought acknowledgment from his followers. *He must have used this phrase a few times before*, Don thought, and indeed, at this most recent pronouncement some of his subordinates appeared to prepare themselves to spring forward.

"He that blasphemes against the Lord," Matt said, "may kisseth a large and hairy ass!"

"Brother," the man said. "I am not familiar with that quote."

"Don, chapter one, verse five," Matt replied. "That there's Don."

The man clenched his fists and roared, moving forward with his toadies close behind. The men on the end of the half-circle jumped the low chain link fence to either side of their intended victims and moved toward the middle where, unwaveringly, Don and Matt prepared themselves for the assault.

Suddenly, the beam of headlights bounced up and over the combatants as a squad car jumped the roadside curb and sped toward them, spinning its tires in the wet grass, siren blasting, red and blue lights flashing. Another cruiser followed the first in line while other law enforcement vehicles could be seen in the distance taking up positions at the perimeters of the park.

An almost comical scene followed as the skinheads, hemmed in by the chain link corridor, attempted to outrun the police cars and gain the open ball diamonds to the north. Their leader tried to climb over the fence but snared the crotch of his jeans on the top wire and had to be rescued from a very uncomfortable straddle as he was apprehended.

In the process of chasing the gang, the police cruisers passed Don and Matt, but a state trooper's cruiser stopped in front of them.

"You can put down that ugly stick now," the state trooper in the second cruiser laughed as he walked up to them. "We'll take it from here."

Don dropped the bat, recognizing the voice and the man as the same person who had stopped them when they turned into the Walmart earlier in the day. The county sheriff and his partner hoisted the two injured boys to their feet and leaned them face down against the hood of their car.

"Thanks," Matt said, taking his hand away from his shoulder and offering it to the trooper. "You got here just in the nick of time."

"Are you hurt?" the trooper asked Matt. "Do you need me to call for medical assistance?"

"No, thanks. I just caught the wrong end of a home run swing by that jerk. I think they'll need medical assistance, though," he added, indicating the young hoodlums with a nod of his head. He extended his left arm a few times over his head and flexed the fingers of his hand. "I think it's just bruised pretty good; nothing's broken."

"If you don't mind," Don said, "could you tell us what's going on here? I mean, I had a totally different impression of this town, what with the security at the Walmart, the gathering in town and all."

"Climb in the car," the trooper said. "I'll take you back to the Walmart. That is where you and your family are camping, correct?"

"I can't believe you remembered us," Matt said.

"It's the truck," the trooper laughed. "Don't see a five-window, fifty-five Chevy in that good shape very often."

Don and Matt talked the trooper into stopping at an all-night diner on the strip before the short drive to the Walmart.

"Perfect time for my late-night break," he offered, as they sat down at a booth. "I'll have to get down to the jail in a little bit after the sheriff and the police round up those *alleged* perpetrators."

After the three men ordered some pie and coffee, Don spoke up.

"So, what's the story? It looks like you all might have coordinated this thing tonight."

"Not much in advance, really. We got word a few days ago that there had been some intimidations and outright assaults at some of the Walmarts along old Route 66 both east and west of here. The law enforcement community – state police, county sheriff, and Elk City police – thought that it all pointed to something coming our way. We had a little meeting about it the night before last and got coordinated in case we had a problem."

"So that's why you were checking travelers in and out of the Walmart?" Matt asked.

"Yep. We figured to be able to spot the troublemakers and at least separate them from the decent folk."

"We certainly had that figured all wrong," Don said.

"It was really for your own protection," the trooper said as the coffee and pies arrived at the booth. "It seems that right now a lot of folks are using that highway heading east from California and staying overnight at Walmarts along the way. Walmart has always been okay with that during the summer vacation months; it represents a lot of sales for them, but it sure does present some potential problems for law enforcement."

"I guess a lot of the campers have been transients or homeless people, huh?" asked Matt.

"That's correct. Of course, Walmart doesn't differentiate between the recreational traveler and the person down on their luck. Normally these types of dustups are just a bunch of local guys blowing off steam. They're out of work fellas who are afraid that the people staying for any length of time in the parking lots are eventually going to take any jobs that are rightfully theirs."

"I think that some people who are feeling pretty low already have to have someone they consider worse off than themselves to pick on sometimes," Matt offered. "I think they're afraid that they, too, might end up homeless and on the road. Makes 'em angry."

"There's that, too," the trooper agreed. "But what happened tonight? Well, that was different."

"How so?" Don asked.

"The organizers of that rally had to get a permit to hold an assembly in the park tonight," the trooper said, "so we knew it was coming off a few days in advance. We figured that it might just turn out to be the catalyst to attract miscreants from outside the community. We felt that the reports coming from Walmarts east into Missouri and west into New Mexico formed a pattern that might eventually collide here."

"So those guys at the rally and the guys that came after us weren't from around here?" Matt asked.

"The guys at the rally and the guys who came after you are one and the same," the trooper said, while forking up his last piece of pie. "After they broke up the rally we waited until they all washed into Red's before we went for them. You just happened to draw them off before we got there. When we get them processed at the jail, I think you'll find they're all from out of the state, or at least way the hell and gone from Elk City."

"Locals wouldn't dare act the way those guys did at the rally," Don added.

"Gives one a bad impression of Elk City, though," Matt said.

"That's true," the trooper said, finishing his coffee. "I grew up here, and it's a great place to be from. Where are you guys headed to?"

"Indiana," Don said. "Our folks pretty much lost everything in the housing crash out in California. We're going back to the old homestead to start over."

"Well, good luck to you on that," the trooper said. "C'mon; let's get you back to your family at the Walmart."

"I'll bet your mom's up wondering where the hell we are," Matt said to Don as they climbed in the cruiser and headed down the highway.

"I could turn on my flashers when we pull up to your camp," the trooper offered.

"Better not," Don said. "My dad would have a heart attack thinking that he was in trouble or something."

"Seems like everybody's had enough excitement for tonight," the trooper chuckled. "With what you've experienced, I'll bet it'll be smooth sailing between here and Indiana."

As they got near the store Don asked the trooper to let them off at the entrance. "I hope so," Don said. "Thanks again for all the help."

"I don't know what we would've done if you hadn't come along when you did," Matt added.

"Just doing my job. You all take care and say a few kind words for Elk City, Oklahoma when you have a chance," and the trooper drove off toward the interstate.

"There's a good guy riding off into the west," Matt said.

18

The first part of the binary catastrophe began as a series of clear, warm days over the waters of the Gulf of Mexico. Boat captains crossed themselves and blessed their luck, for such fine weather meant that they would fill every bunk of their three and five-day fishing charters. The water was warm, and the bait fish were schooling closer to shore - great black balls of rotating, flashing saltwater fodder - attracting amberjack, tuna, sailfish, dorado, and the highly prized blue marlin.

The sun sparkled and warmed the surface waters of the sea, and the air began to rise and move toward the Texas shore as scattered, light surface breezes that did nothing to cool the sunburned faces of the fishermen. The clear days persisted. What began as an invisible, insensate, thermodynamic consequence of natural processes eventually formed what meteorologists on the evening news would later identify as a warm air mass, heavily laden with moisture, bowed in the middle along its nine hundred mile front, pushing up into the center of the country. Friction along the surface of the land and the earth's rotation caused the mass to begin a slow deflection to the east in a phenomenon known as the *Coriolis Effect*.

About the same time – in the atmosphere above the Canadian forests - a cool air mass began a southern migration driven by the high-altitude jet stream. This was the second component of the impending disaster. Still a few days away from its consummation with the warmer Gulf air over the central plains of Kansas, this cold front fell down to the earth's surface and began moving eastward. Isobaric charts at the National Oceanographic and Atmospheric Administration facility in Fort Peck, Montana and at the National Weather Service Forecast Office in Norman, Oklahoma graphically indicated the temperature, direction, and speed of the approaching cold front. But people in the Great Plains – living barometers accustomed to the seasonal variation and flux of weather systems – did not need an inexact science to inform them that tornado season had arrived.

As the great bubble of warm Gulf air bulged slowly from the south, organisms on the ground experienced the high temperature and humidity compressed beneath it. Wood thrush and other birds of the fields' edge started their circadian songs in the coolness of early morning. But as the low, brush-filtered light metamorphosed into sharp-angled yellow energy, heavy and humid air clotted the shade and liquid birdsong yielded to the relentless dry drone of insects.

For the inhabitants of the northern plains, these clear days and gentle breezes of low pressure were a welcomed respite from winter's harshness. For those who suffered in the forge of southern high-pressure systems, there was a sense that a slow, unseen menace was passing overhead. In the northwest winds of the Dakotas, the green seed heads of winter wheat weather vaned toward the inevitable junction of these two systems. In Texas, farm workers sweated, turned their faces from the sky and bent their backs in labor while cumulus clouds – formed from moisture condensing as warm air rose and cooled – were swept northward into the inevitable friction of air masses: death on the wind.

19

Sunday, May 22, 2011. A line of clouds was building to the north as the family caravan tracked eastward along Interstate 40 toward Oklahoma City. Don was in the lead driving the Chevy truck with his mother riding along with him. Matt – in the back seat nursing his sore shoulder – rode with Uncle Kenny and Paige; Tom brought up the rear, pulling the tent trailer with Jenny and Julie in the back seat, Scout riding up front. A stiff crosswind was blowing from the south, but the morning air was so humid that the two newer trucks had their air conditioners on. The older Chevy was manufactured without such comforts. Even with both windows down, the heat in the cab was stifling.

"Are you okay to drive?" Elizabeth asked. "You didn't get much sleep last night."

"I'm fine for now," Don replied, "but I might need a break later this afternoon."

"That might be a good reason to stop a little earlier today. We were all up late last night."

"I think we're gonna hit some weather today, Mom. See those build-ups? By afternoon they're gonna turn into thunderheads. Wouldn't surprise me if we didn't see some hail along with it."

"I was hoping we'd make Springfield, Missouri by this evening. But if it starts raining it'll probably also be windy; I don't think we should take a chance with the trailers. What do you think?"

"I'd agree; we're making good time. Once we get out of Oklahoma, the country's not as wide open anyway. There'll be plenty of little towns and places to stop for the night as we go along through Missouri. We'll be at the farm tomorrow night - Tuesday night at the latest."

Mother and son continued the small talk for a few more minutes. Finally, Elizabeth got around to the reason she insisted on riding with Don that morning.

"Donnie," she began. "I need to ask you something."

"Go ahead, Mom," he replied smiling. "I figured you'd get around to it sooner or later. We didn't have much of a debrief last night – or should I say - earlier this morning."

"Did they hurt you, Donnie? It looks like Matt took a pretty good beating to his arm; what about you?"

"Never got touched," Don laughed. "Matt yelled at me, and I ducked - but that's when he got nailed on his arm by the baseball bat. He's lucky it ain't broke, but I guess I'm luckier. If it would've caught me upside the head, I'd probably be dead."

"But you're not hurt?" Elizabeth continued. "I heard what you did to those two that attacked you. That wasn't a result of some pent-up anger, or what do they call it, post-traumatic stress disorder?"

Don laughed so hard he had to wipe the tears out of his eyes. He looked over at his mother and saw that her eyes were wide in disbelief.

"No, Mom. What happened last night was a result of someone trying to take my head off, not some post-war trauma. I just reacted the way I was trained."

"But I thought you weren't in combat, just interrogation."

"That's true, but I went through basic like everyone else. And in-country, we have regular drills and exercises to keep our edge. All I did was a little hand-to-hand combat technique."

"But there were two of them! What if they'd had guns?"

"They were kids, Mom, kids. I doubt that they're old enough to have graduated from high school yet. I figure that I cracked that one kid's ribs – sure did feel like it. The other one's gonna need some knee surgery for sure. I shouldn't have done that - but it all happened so quickly."

"Matt told me last night that a much larger group of men were just about to jump you, and if that would've happened, the outcome would have been very different."

"There's no doubt about that. We were very fortunate that the cops came along when they did. That trooper told us that the town's been anticipating some sort of trouble for the last few days; Matt and I just happened to walk into the middle of it."

"I just don't know what this world is coming to," Elizabeth said. "It just seems like there's no civility left in people. I don't want my children growing up in a world of anarchists!"

"Mom don't let a couple of strange coincidences throw you off. Those guys back in New Mexico and those people last night were aberrations. It does seem like things in the country are not real good right now; I don't know – I've been away too long. But compared to the situation I've been in for the last few years, this is tame."

"It seems to me that it's the situation – not the people - in this country that's bad," his mother replied. "But we've got to stay clear of the bad; that's why getting back to our Indiana roots is so important. Your little brother and the twins - we must make something decent for them to hang on to when it starts getting worse, and I'm convinced it's going to get worse before it gets better. Us older folks, we have a memory of better times – the younger folks, they don't."

"That's probably why those two kids attacked us. They have no idea where they're headed and look to that gang of adults for guidance – if you want to call it that. It's pretty much the same situation in Afghanistan or Iraq; it's the reason young people become suicide bombers in the Middle East or take up rifles in Africa. Kids are so susceptible to manipulation at that age, mostly because they want to fit in."

"You've seen this overseas?"

"Mom, it'd break your heart. Most of the suicide bombers are teenagers – boys mostly – but in the last few years, they've been recruiting girls as well. Groups like Al Qaeda convince them that they'll go directly to heaven as martyrs. Considering how their life really sucks – especially if they live in refugee camps – it doesn't take much convincing."

Kenny, Matt, and Paige were leading the little convoy down the road.

"You awake back there?" Uncle Kenny asked, looking in the rear-view mirror mounted on his windshield.

"Just dozing a little bit," Matt replied, adjusting the ice bag on his injured arm.

"Hand me up the bag, and I'll put more ice in it," Paige offered.

Unfastening her belt, she turned in her seat and knelt, facing backwards, leaning on the seatback with her elbows. When Matt removed the ice bag, Paige could see the large purple bruise and knot that swelled on his arm; her eyes opened wide in admiration, and she blushed. Her father shifted his eyes from the mirror to his daughter and smiled. Paige took the bag and twisted back around to a sitting position. She unscrewed the plastic cap and poured the melt water inside it into a small cooler, replacing it with ice cubes. Then she refastened the cap and turned back to Matt, pressing the bag against her forearm to shape the cold compress of cubes before gently placing it against Matt's biceps.

"Does that hurt very much?" she asked.

"Not now, thanks," Matt smiled, holding her questioning gaze for a few unnerving moments before she turned away, self-conscious of a rising excitement that caught her by surprise. After a few miles, her father broke the silence.

"I'm sure glad you boys didn't have to stay around to bring charges against those hoodlums," Uncle Kenny said as they neared Oklahoma City.

"No need; they were in enough trouble already," Matt said, flexing his injured biceps. "That trooper told us that when they took those guys into custody, most of them already had a rap sheet as long as their arm."

"The ones that don't have a record will probably be held for a few days on charges of being drunk and disorderly or some other misdemeanor," Uncle Kenny said. "If they can pay their fines, they'll take 'em to the edge of town and turn 'em loose. Not much else they can do."

"Normally, I'd say we need to keep a lookout for the ones they're turning loose," Matt offered. "The trooper said that they're transients themselves. But I figure we'll be off the road and back in Indiana by the time they're out."

"What about the two that attacked you?" Paige asked.

"It'll be a while for those two; I figure that they got the worst of it," Matt laughed. "Don put his boot into that one kid's ribs and the other might need a knee replacement down the road."

"They're probably young enough to be remanded to their parents' custody," Uncle Kenny said. "I wonder if at least the father wasn't one of the older members of the gang."

"What did the gang look like?" Paige asked in wonderment. "I can imagine that they were pretty scary looking. Were they tattooed?"

"Hard to tell because it was mostly dark, but you know," Matt laughed, "when their heads are shaved and they're coming at you, they all pretty much look alike."

"Looks like you kids are going to get to see some real weather by this afternoon," Tom said to his children.

The twins – as was their habit - were in the back seat of the truck in secret counsel with each other, whispering softly and occasionally glancing up at Scout in the front seat. Sometimes they would giggle at some pretended confidence because they knew it would irritate their little brother. Their father was familiar with the game, and he smiled, knowing it would be a few years before Scout would catch on; but right now, he tried to distract his pouting son.

"You see those puffy clouds?" Tom said. "Those are called cumulus clouds, formed by the sun heating the earth's surface. Since warm air is lighter than cold air, it rises, and if the air is moist, the water vapor condenses into a cloud; if it keeps getting warmer, later this afternoon they'll probably grow to be pretty tall, then they're called cumulonimbus clouds."

In a concerted effort to ignore his sisters, Scout joined in the conversation.

"Do you think it'll rain, Dad?" Scout asked. "Do you think we might see some tornados?"

"Oh, I think we'll see rain, but tornados? That's hard to say," his father answered. "This area of the country is known as *Tornado Alley*.

Your mother and I listened to the forecast last night, and there's warm air coming up from the Gulf of Mexico and cool air moving in behind us; that's the makings of a tornado. They're predicting thunderstorms all along the line where those two systems meet. It's called the *dry line*. We'll either be one side or the other of it when we stop in Springfield, Missouri tonight."

"Will we be safe in the tent?" Jenny asked.

"We'll be just fine," her father answered. "In general, if there's any really bad weather, it'll be over by evening. That's because once the sun's down, there's no more heating of the earth; the clouds don't grow; and their energy is dissipated in the form of rain."

The family drove along in silence for a few more miles, the children looking out the truck windows, studying the line of developing cumulonimbus intently.

"Those clouds seem to be growing bigger," Scout said, leaning forward to look under the edge of the truck's roof. "I've been watching that one right out there. How far away do you think it is, Daddy?" he asked, pointing past the windshield to the northeast.

"Oh, I'd say it's about a hundred miles at least, and you're right; it's growing pretty good. In fact, if you look there seems to be a whole series of 'em marching to the northeast. That must mark the position of that dry line I was talking about."

"It looks pretty dark underneath and I think I can see some rain," Julie offered. "But the rain doesn't seem to be reaching the ground."

"Probably just cloud shadow," her father said. "But it could also be virga – that's rain that doesn't reach the ground – or also hail."

"Whoa!" Scout cried. "Did you see that lightning up top?"

"Nothing to worry about. You kids probably haven't seen much lightning growing up in California. And thunder? Just wait until we get to the farm. There's a metal roof on the barn. There's nothing better than going to sleep in the hay loft with the sound of rain on the roof and the rumble of thunder off in the distance."

"Are we headed to where those clouds are?" Scout asked.

"Those clouds look like they're sliding to the northeast," his father answered. "We'll probably miss them."

"But what if we drive into them?" Jenny asked.

"Yeah," Julie added. "What if instead of going north they decide to come south to where we're headed. Are we going to cross paths with some serious weather?"

"Unlikely," Tom replied. "Thunderstorms only last about thirty minutes; after that they dissipate. By the time we get to where those clouds are now, the most we'll probably get is a light rain."

As he made his pronouncement, the distant clouds continued to build, leaving Tom to wonder whether they might develop into super cells, the incubators of tornados. *If there is to be severe weathe*r, he thought, *it'd be best to stop behind the front and get a fresh start in the morning.* Rather than try to make Springfield tonight, at their next gas stop, he'd speak with Kenny and Elizabeth and suggest the group stop early in Joplin. *After all, it is Sunday,* he thought, *a day of rest.*

20

The "dry line" is invisible because it is a meteorological construct of men's minds. It is first given shape and form when small flags are placed on weather maps to indicate the direction of winds and their speeds. Appearing like musical notes, these pennants dance between lines that connect areas of similar temperature or pressure. Also known as the *dew point line*, the dry line separates moist air coming up out of the Gulf of Mexico from dry air moving eastward from the desert southwest. The dry line is thought to be an important factor in the frequency of severe weather in the Great Plains of North America. Oriented generally north-to-south, it can stretch from the High Plains of the United States to the Canadian Prairie.

Maps are two-dimensional representations of physical phenomenon, modern computer modeling can produce three-dimensional images with motion that help scientists predict the movement of weather systems, but the real action takes place in a vertical dimension beginning near the surface of the earth. Along the dry line, cool air wedges under the less-dense warmer air and lifts it. This upward motion causes the formation of clouds. When enough moisture is present, a line of showers and thunderstorms occurs, reaching their greatest intensity along the dry line. On weather maps, a cold front is indicated by a blue line of triangles pointing in the direction they are traveling. At the surface, the temperature drops on the leading edge of a cold front and winds shift clockwise from southwest to northwest in a process known as *veering*. It is the collision of warm air and cool air along the dry line that creates tornados.

Tornadoes form within severe thunderstorms as warm air rises and cool air falls in a vertical, cyclonic effect. Some scientists believe that it is the forward movement of a weather system that tilts this vertical circulation, producing the horizontal winds that create a tornado.

There are a lot of theories about tornadoes but this much is true: though they can be found throughout the world, most of them occur in the United States in an area known as *Tornado Alley*. They are difficult to study because they don't last very long – usually less than fifteen minutes – which makes them hard to predict as well.

A tornado's energy is concentrated in a relatively small area, and scientists must wait until a tornado has passed before they can assess how strong it was; in other words, the size of a tornado has no bearing on its strength, so it's impossible to predict damage in advance of the storm. In 2001, a man named Fujita developed a system that ranks tornadoes based on the damage they ultimately cause. Revised in 2007, this system is known by meteorologists as the Enhanced Fujita Tornado Scale, or *EF Scale*. The EF Scale is comprised of six damage categories that range from zero to five, with an EF5 tornado causing the highest degree of destruction.

Strange manifestations have followed the passage of tornadoes across the landscape. While the remains of one home might be comprised of only its cleanly-swept foundation, the house next door might survive untouched. There are the heartbreaking stories of people who survived by clustering in closets, while friends - in their tornado-proof shelters - were sucked away to a disfiguring death. Photos exist of intact wooden two-by-fours impaled in cinder block walls and garden hoses driven through the living trunks of trees. A story from Kansas relates how a barn was dismantled by a twister, but horses that were inside were set down, unharmed a few miles away, still tethered to the same hitching post. And of course, everyone knows the story of Dorothy Gale and the *Wizard of Oz*.

April of 2011 was the most active month for tornadoes on record. In the final week of that month, more than three hundred people were killed by an extreme tornado outbreak in the Great Plains. In comparison, the first three weeks of May were relatively quiet, marked by only a few isolated thunderstorms. But the inhabitants of Tornado Alley, knowing better than any meteorologist the environment in which they lived, watched and waited as an area of low pressure approached from the west – accompanied by its breezy, clear skies, a dry line, and a cold front – and pushed eastward toward warm air bulging up from the Gulf of Mexico.

On Saturday, May 21, 2011, thunderstorms began to develop over Brown County in the northeastern part of Kansas. A tornado appearing to be of low intensity - except to the people on the ground, of course – first caused minor damage in Topeka but later resulted in major damage in Oskaloosa and other towns as the system moved eastward. At about the same time a system of thunderstorms southeast of Emporia spawned an EF3 tornado in Reading that destroyed twenty homes, killed one person, and injured several others. In the aftermath of those dissipating storm systems, only a moderate risk for severe weather was issued for much of the Midwest on the following day: Sunday, May 22, 2011.

21

By Sunday afternoon - at the family's last fuel stop near Claremore, Oklahoma - the sky had become ominously darker to the north of the caravan's easterly track along the Will Rogers Parkway. In council, the adults had decided that Tom should lead and make the decision as to when the little group would pull over for the night. Their decision was based on a level of comfort all had with Tom's self-professed knowledge of weather. He had once taken an aeronautical ground school course and routinely opined: "Meteorological prognostication is one of the chief virtues of a good pilot!" But in truth everyone agreed that the truck pulling the pop-up tent trailer was the least aerodynamically stable of all the vehicles in the group and could therefore function as a barometer for safety.

The twins had moved into Uncle Kenny's truck with Paige; Matt decided that he should stop at the next hospital to get his shoulder x-rayed, and the map showed there was a medical center in the Joplin area. He felt fine enough to drive the Chevy, so Don rode along with him intending to catch a nap for the last few hours of travel. Elizabeth and Scout rode with Tom.

"I surely wish we'd had time to see the Will Rogers' Monument and Museum," Elizabeth said. "But in truth, I think if we'd taken the time for that we'd probably be staying in Claremore tonight."

"Kind of a shame, really," Tom said. "I think the kids would've gotten a lot out of it. I heard there is a one-of-a-kind gun collection there."

"Never met a man he didn't like," Scout added from the back seat.

"How'd you know that?" his father asked.

"We read about him in school. I'll bet he wouldn't have said that about those guys last night in Elk City."

"I think what he was trying to say," his mother replied, "is that we should look for the good in everyone, not just the bad."

"I don't see much good in those clouds off to the left," Tom said warily. "Maybe we should have stayed in Claremore for the night and let this system pass."

"Let's just find the Walmart in Joplin and stop there," Elizabeth said. "It's not yet four o'clock, and we'll have plenty of time to get set up before dark."

After paying their tolls at the Kansas border, the family crossed into Missouri on Interstate 44.

"According to the map, the next Walmart's off exit 8," Elizabeth said, "just a few miles north of the interstate on Range Line Road."

"We might as well stop there, 'cause we sure ain't gonna outrun this storm," Tom said as he turned on his emergency flashers for a few seconds, the pre-arranged signal to the others that they should pull over to the road shoulder.

Don and Kenny ran forward through the rising wind to the family council at the lead truck. Elizabeth rolled down her window as they approached on the lee side of truck.

"Kenny," Tom said as the truck was rocked by the gusty west wind. "The Walmart's a few exits up the road. I figure we should get our oil changed while we're there this evening."

"That's a good idea," Kenny replied loudly. "Mine's due - and if we can get us a bay in the shop, it'll keep the trucks and trailers out of this storm."

"The map says there's a hospital called St. John's in Joplin," Don said. "I figure Matt and I'll head there first to get his arm x-rayed. We'll join up with you afterwards but don't wait dinner on us, though. It's a hospital and may be a while before we get waited on."

A few miles later, as the caravan made its way off the interstate and through the eastern outskirts of the city, Don and Matt turned at a blue "H" roadside sign indicating the direction of the hospital. As the remaining vehicles continued north up Range Line Road, a wedge of dark clouds seemed to have descended over the city.

When Tom and Kenny pulled behind the Walmart to the auto center, Kenny jumped out of his truck and ran into the service counter. In a few minutes he reappeared.

"The manager said for both of us to pull on in," Kenny said. "We don't need to drop the trailers, either; he figure's it'll take about an hour or so."

The two brothers parked their truck-trailer tandems in parallel bays as the service technicians pulled the overhead doors down against the approaching storm. The inside of the store seemed eerily quiet.

"Tom," Elizabeth said as each truck unloaded its passengers. "We passed a pizza place on the way in. It's just across the parking lot over there," she added indicating the direction of the restaurant by pointing toward the front of the store with her hand. "Why don't you order a few pies for dinner? We'll join you over there when we're done. Scout, you go along and help your father."

"What about them?" Scout asked.

"The girls and I need to pick up some things in here," his mother replied.

Scout's sisters looked at him and smiled mysteriously then turned to follow their mother and Paige into the store's interior.

"I'll come with you guys," Uncle Kenny said to Tom.

Elizabeth and the girls were in the pharmacy department in the southwest corner of the Walmart picking out their personal items; Tom, Kenny, and Scout were in the parking lot outside the Pizza Hut watching the approaching squall line, and Matt and Don had just entered the emergency room at St. John's hospital when the tornado warning sirens sounded.

22

At around 5:08 p.m. storm spotters reported seeing multiple funnel clouds in Cherokee county, Kansas due west of Joplin, prompting an alert from the National Weather Service in Springfield, Missouri. Tornado sirens in Joplin were sounded at 5:17 p.m. A supercell thunderstorm intensified rapidly. At 5:25 p.m. a funnel cloud was spotted on the ground near Riverton on the Kansas/Missouri border.

"It was clear that a hook echo was forming and that a large tornado was developing," Mike Griffith, a meteorologist with the weather service station would say later. "We picked up a debris ball here on our radar. When you see that, it signifies that major damage is going on."

Bill Davis, the Meteorologist in Charge of the Springfield, Missouri National Weather Service Station prepared an event review that describes the movement of the storm:

"Storm chasers and spotters reported seeing multiple vortices rotating around the parent circulation near the beginning of this tornado. This was documented by various video and photos from several locations, and through eyewitness and spotter reports. Once the tornado became rain wrapped, it would have been difficult to discern if multiple vortices continued to be present at the most intense portion of the tornado's life cycle."

"There's lightning... there's hail!"
"Get the sirens goin'! Get the sirens goin'!"
"It's comin' down right here."
"The trees are debarked!"
"I can smell it!"

"As the tornado crossed Schifferdecker Avenue just south of Sunset Drive, it widened more and increased in intensity. The forward speed of the tornado through most of Joplin was about 20 to 25 miles per hour. The tornado continued east northeast crossing 29th and Winfield Avenue. Numerous homes, businesses, and medical arts buildings were destroyed by EF-4 to low end EF-5 wind speeds. Numerous vehicles of various sizes and weight were tossed across or from parking lots and driveways. Steel framed roofs were lifted and wrapped around trees and objects. Some vehicles were crushed or flattened and wrapped around trees. Concrete constructed walls were toppled and moved several feet or crushed into foundations."

"It's going to cross the road right there!"
"Don't get us into it!"
"Be quiet, I'm not!"
"Don't get us into it… don't get us into it!"
"Shut up! Shut up!"
"I am! Don't get us into it!"

"Did you hear that?" Matt asked as the two young men walked into the empty emergency room at the St. John's Hospital.

"Tornado sirens!" Don said as he headed back to the front door. "You check in; I'm going outside for a minute."

But before Don could reach the doors, an abrasive buzzer began to echo inside the hospital, accompanied by a calm, recorded voice intoning: "Execute Code Grey… Execute Code Grey." From behind the counter, a nurse called out to Don and Matt.

"Quickly!" she cried. "We need your help with the patients. There's a tornado coming!"

The two looked at each other in amazement and immediately jumped over the counter to follow the nurse down a corridor where the lights were already beginning to flicker. The nurse entered a room on the left, and they followed. In the ward there were half a dozen people on beds, some with intravenous tubes attached to them while others were hooked up to diagnostic machines. The roar of the wind outside the hospital began to increase in intensity, and the windows began to flex inward then outward as the pressure differential oscillated with the approaching tornado.

"Take the head of the bed!" the nurse cried as she released the gurney's wheel brakes. "You!" she said to Matt, "keep up with the IV stand. We've got to get them into the hallway and away from the windows!"

They wheeled the first patient to safety, then the second, and a third. Each time they went back into the ward to retrieve another bed, the outside air became darker, and the wail of the approaching tornado grew louder. As they pushed the last bed through the hallway door, Don looked out of the rattling windows and was shocked to see a wide column of murky, horizontally rotating debris coming across the parking lot. As if in slow motion, cars were being lifted and thrown before the black mass, disappearing in the forward movement of the twister. In the hallway, the nurse had covered each of the patients' heads with their blankets and had thrown herself across one patient's body. Matt and Don followed her example just as the edge of the debris wave hit the hospital, knocking the entire building off its foundation. The lights went out leaving the hallway a screeching blackness.

Don felt his ears pop as the air inside the corridor was first compressed then released in a sucking motion. He had draped himself over an old man on the hospital bed, clasping the railing at the bed's edge and wedging his feet into the frame on the other side. Although he appeared unconscious, Don could feel the old man's heartbeat against his own chest.

"Cover your heads!" was the last thing he heard the nurse scream as invisible shards of glass - blasted inward from the windows - scoured the hallway, cutting exposed flesh. In the sharp, particulate maelstrom, Don sensed soft, shapeless masses passing behind him through the corridor and into nothingness.

> *"At St. John's, numerous vehicles of various sizes and weight were tossed several hundred yards. Some vehicles were crushed beyond recognition. Some of the St. John's medical staff and other people*

along the core tornado path could not locate their vehicles. A large St. John's medical vehicle was tossed across the parking lot and landed north of 26th Street. Also, their life flight helicopter was blown off the roof and destroyed.

"The St. John's Hospital structure had just about every window blown out on three sides. Once the wind was inside the building, it caused severe destruction of interior walls and ceilings on every floor. A portion of the top roof was removed or heavily damaged. It was reported by structural engineers that a portion of the hospital's foundation and underpinning system were compromised. The engineers determined the entire structure was not safe and would have to be demolished and replaced with a new structure."

Tom, Kenny, and Scout were standing in the parking lot of the Pizza Hut when what appeared to be a horizontal cloud of rolling dust plunged at them from the west. The manager of the Pizza Hut rushed out of his building and called to everyone watching the storm.

"Inside everyone!" he cried. "It's a tornado – you need to be inside. C'mon!"

Tom and Scout joined a dozen people who rushed through the doors of the restaurant, unaware that Kenny had taken off running toward the front of the Walmart to reach it before the storm hit.

Inside the Pizza Hut, the manager quickly directed the crowd into a freezer in the back of the store. With all the bodies jammed inside, the manager had difficulty getting the large metal door to latch. He took a bungee cord and wrapped it first around the door handle and then his arm, pulling the door as tightly shut as he could.

As the tornado crushed the building, the suction began to pull at the heavy metal door. Tom tried to grab the manager by his waist to help keep the door closed but as the wind screamed to its highest decibel, the door was wrenched from its hinges, and was sucked into the vortex – taking the manager with it like a key on a kite string.

"The main force of the three-quarter mile wide tornado, centered between 26th and East 20th Streets, continued its destruction of buildings. A bank was totally destroyed with exterior concrete walls swept from the foundation. The only thing left of the bank was the slightly damaged steel and concrete bank vault. To the east of the bank, two story apartments were leveled into piles. The Dillon's grocery store had significant roof and exterior wall damage. Over 30 people took shelter near the back of the store in one of the freezers."

As a contractor, Kenny had a hand in constructing a few Walmarts, and he understood the flimsy nature of their warehouse-like design. As he raced across the parking lot toward the front of the store, he felt a small piece of debris strike his shoulder. He looked up to his left to see an over-arching black anvil of cloud and dust that appeared ready to fall on the Walmart. He turned his attention back to the store, now less than one hundred feet away and directly in the path of the onrushing, circling surge of debris. With eyes that only a father has for his daughter, he saw Paige standing near the front window. Stumbling, he tried to gesture for her to back away to the inside of the building, but the air was sucked out of his lungs as he was lifted off his feet and propelled into the heart of the cyclone. The image of his daughter would be his last memory. Mercifully, he was knocked unconscious by a piece of debris before his body was torn apart inside the twister.

Inside the Walmart, the storm was not noticeable at first, but as the debris started appearing in the parking lot and the sound of large objects falling on the roof became more frequent and louder, the shoppers inside began to move to the front of the building, where the windows directly faced the approaching tornado. They stood transfixed in disbelief as the dark, inhuman force moved inevitably in their direction, less than a quarter mile away. There was nowhere to hide. Over the intercom, the manager announced that people needed to move quickly away from the windows and into the interior of the building to take shelter.

Among this group stood Paige, rooted in fear, her eyes searching the far end of the parking lot. For a moment she thought she saw her father running toward her but then the image disappeared in the dust and horizontal rain sweeping the parking lot. A strong hand gripped her shoulder.

"Paige!" her Aunt Elizabeth cried. "You've got to come with me – hurry!"

Elizabeth pulled her niece back into the anticipated safety of the darkened interior. The parallel merchandise aisles were perpendicular to the long axis of the building, directly in line with the approaching tornado. Elizabeth's quick thinking reasoned that if the windows blew out, all the deadly debris would be channeled directly into these aisles. She shepherded the girls to the southwest corner of the building where concrete walls on the front and side of the building came together in a ninety-degree angle of safety. As she pushed the girls toward that poor, lone refuge, Elizabeth had each of them grab rolled-up thermal blankets from a display at the end of an aisle.

"Cover your heads with these!" she commanded as they crouched together against the block wall - debris beginning to swirl around them. The twins were alternately screaming and sobbing, but the sounds of their voices were lost in the roar of the storm. Paige closed her eyes tightly, choked back her sobs and did not cry out, even as a large display case toppled over on top of them, pinning them to the floor.

"Along most of the primary damage track, it was very common to find various size boards, limbs, and even small twigs and leaves embedded into wood and stucco walls. In some cases, even cardboard was embedded sideways into stucco walls. This was common at the high school. At one spot, a two by four board was driven right through a concrete curb without breaking.

"The wood framing from most homes disintegrated into small pieces. This caused thousands of deadly projectiles. Many open fields were covered with boards, limbs, twigs, and other materials, including steel beams, and fencing that were embedded deeply into

the ground like tossed spears. At one location, the four legs of a wooden chair had been embedded into a stucco wall without being damaged."

"They said there's one on the ground headed this way!"
"Where do you want me to put everyone?"
"How many?"
"At least ten adults.... I don't know how many kids."
"Everybody, get down! Low on the ground!"
(Crash)
"It's okay, it's okay!"
(Wind)
"I can't hear!"
"Ohh!"
(Sound of fine debris hitting walls)
"Heavenly Father! Jesus! Jesus!"
"We're good, we're good, we're okay!"
"Heavenly Father! Jesus! Jesus!"
"I love you guys!"
"We're gonna be okay.... We're gonna be okay!"
"Daddy! Daddy!"
"Thank you, Jesus! Thank you, Jesus!"
"Somebody's on my back!"
"Sorry, sorry.... I can't move just yet..."
"Stay calm, stay calm..."
"I think that's the end of it..."

"The tornado continued eastward between 22nd and 20th Streets where it crossed Connecticut Avenue. The severe damage continued to mount with hundreds more homes and businesses heavily damaged or destroyed. When the tornado reached South Rangeline Road and 20th, one of Joplin's main business sections, it destroyed several well-constructed buildings along with the Sports Academy, Walmart, Home Depot, the Pepsi Distribution center, Cummins generator

building, a large construction firm located east of the Home Depot, and tore apart a large three-story apartment complex east of Walmart. Two large cell towers were toppled northward on top of a portion of the apartment complex. A couple of the Walmart tractor trailers were tossed over 200 yards on top of the debris of what was left of the Pepsi Distribution center.

"A parking lot west of the Home Depot, and a portion of the Walmart parking lot had scoured asphalt. Vehicles parked in the Home Depot parking lot were tossed several hundred yards, one into the Home Depot. Across and east of Interstate 44 and to where the tornado lifted about 4.8 miles north northeast of Granby, Missouri, the tornado continued to damage homes, mobile homes, outbuildings, and to topple trees. At this last portion of the track, the tornado was about 500 yards wide and produced low end EF-1 to EF-0 damage.

"Estimated through May 31, 2011, 6,954 homes were destroyed, 359 homes had major damage, and 516 homes had minor damage. Numerous small to large businesses were either destroyed or damaged. Several public buildings were either destroyed or damaged. This included several churches, elementary schools, high school, vocational school, two fire stations, a Walmart, Home Depot, large construction company with heavy equipment, nursing home, banks, a Dillon's and other grocery stores, several gas station/convenience stores, Cummins generator building, electric power company sub-station, major cell and power transmission towers, and numerous one, two, and three level apartment buildings."

"Oh, God; there's little kids in the back of that car, turn around, turn around!"

"Where? Where?"

"Back there! Turn around!"

"They're coming out of the car! Stop, stop! Let me out!"

"Are you okay are you okay?"
"Are you alright? Sit down right here, right there..."
"I hear people... someone's in there; hello? Hello?"
"Oh, Lord, Oh, Lord... it's crushed, it's... it's... their..."
(Sobbing).
"Here. Boy.... come here, boy..."
"He's shaking... he's scared..."
"I think he was in the car.... come here, boy!"
"Watch it, he might bite you!"
"Come here, boy..."

In a brief span of thirty-eight minutes, the Joplin tornado – three-quarters of a mile wide at its apex – traveled a little over twenty-two miles, killed one hundred sixty people and caused an estimated $2.8 billion damage. As the storm system passed and night began to fall, a light rain cloaked the community as rescuers began to search for survivors and recover the dead.

23

As the roar of the wind subsided, a fine film of dust choked the darkness. Stunned and semi-conscious, Don was unaware of the passage of time except through the throbbing of the patient's heart on the hospital bed beneath him. After a while he sensed that the man's lifeblood had found a rupture through which it could pass unchecked. Don felt the pounding of the heart increase to where it seemed that it would burst out of the man's chest; then it suddenly faded and after a few moments, disappeared altogether. The old man took one final, rattling breath and lay still. With his arms and legs still wedged into the bed's framework, Don lifted his head and saw the rain-sparkled light growing through the shattered doorframe and started to cry.

Matt woke up in a darkened room at the end of the hallway unsure of where he was or what had happened. He was lying on the floor, his back to a wall with the mattress of the hospital bed pressed against the length his body. As his awareness grew, Matt began to struggle against his confinement, pushing the mattress and bedframe with his arms and legs. He managed to move them enough to free himself from the compressive squeeze. Pulling himself upward off the floor, he looked over the edge of his protective prison at a pile of debris as tall as a man and composed of doors, window frames, and undefined pieces of wood, strips of carpet, floor tiles, ceiling panels, and plaster. He became aware of the ache in his injured shoulder, but that hurt now seemed minor compared to the pain that began to spread throughout the rest of his body.

A light was growing in the hallway on the other side of the room. *I must have rolled and tumbled down that corridor*, Matt thought as he climbed cautiously over the debris to the doorway. *That bed and mattress were the only thing that saved me.* Reaching the hallway, he looked back into the room. The west-facing windows had been driven inward, and their frames were distorted. A light rain began to blow into the room, settling the dust. Matt stared at the appalling pile of rubble he had just crossed and wondered: *What happened to the patient on the bed?* He shuddered, realizing that person was probably wrapped in the winding sheets of his hospital bedding, entombed beneath the wreckage.

At the pizza restaurant, when the wind ripped the freezer door and the store manager from the building, Tom had thrown his arms around Scout and gripped one of the frames inside the freezer, compressing them both against the force of the storm. It was enough. After the maelstrom had passed, the survivors staggered out from inside the freezer into a yellowish haze full of paper-like debris swirling and falling around them like the inside of a snow-globe.

"Are you okay?" Tom asked, giving his son a quick inspection with his eyes while running his hands over the boy's arms and legs, turning his head gently to check for injuries.

"I'm okay," Scout replied shakily. "Where's Uncle Kenny?"

"You sit down on the curb there," Tom commanded, looking around the scene of destruction. "I'll go look for him."

"We'll watch your boy until you get back," an older couple offered. "We ain't goin' nowhere for a while."

"Thanks, I'll be back in a few minutes."

Tom ran toward the Walmart, the front windows now glassless, hollow-eyed, and dark. As he closed the distance to the building, he scanned the parking lot, looking for signs of his brother. The asphalt had been sheared from the parking lot like veneer; the heavy concrete parking dividers – six feet long and weighing hundreds of pounds – had been lifted off their rebar restraints, pulled into the air and driven back to earth, spiked into the ground like tent stakes. Tom stopped, looked to the east at the receding storm, and somehow knew.

After a few moments, he made his way past shoppers that were staggering out of the building with hideous injuries and between bodies that had already been placed in the parking lot and covered with any available blanket, sheet or tablecloth. In the light rain, the fabric clung to the prone, motionless forms, giving them shape. Tom headed toward the back of the store, to the automotive department, reasoning that wherever Elizabeth and the girls might have been at the time the storm hit, they would eventually make their way back to the vehicles – if the trucks were still there. He shut out the thought that any of them might lay beneath the dark, reddening shrouds in the parking lot.

The air conditioning units had been ripped from the roof of the building allowing light as well as rain to penetrate the interior. It was eerily quiet inside as all motion and sound from the front of the store seemed to diminish as Tom descended into the dim, wet interior. He navigated the overturned racks and merchandise flotsam, stopping only to call out his wife's name and listen. After a few minutes of desperate effort, he reached the service bays. One of the doors had been torn away from behind the Airstream trailer on the far side of the garage allowing light to penetrate the area. Amazingly, both trucks and trailers appeared to have been spared from the worst of the storm.

Tom was about to turn around and begin searching the rest of the store when he heard voices coming from inside the Airstream. He moved stiffly between the tongue of the trailer and his truck, not sure of what he might find. The trailer door was open, and there on the step sat Paige, looking blank and unfocused. Inside the trailer he heard his wife's strong voice:

"You take this washcloth and take turns cleaning off each other's face," she commanded the twins. "I've got to look after your cousin."

"Elizabeth!" he cried out. "Are you okay?" He walked over to the door of the trailer just as his wife stepped down, greeting him with a weak hug and a smile that disappeared as quickly as it was formed.

"Where's Scout?" she asked quietly.

"He's across the lot, and he's okay," Tom replied. "Some folks are looking after him 'til I get back."

Elizabeth looked back at Paige, who remained motionless in the door of the trailer. Before she could ask, Tom raised his hand in a cautionary expression and, without words, shook his head briefly from side to side. Elizabeth nodded and went to her niece. Gathering the young girl into her arms, Elizabeth led Paige toward her father's truck. Tom opened the back door, and the couple laid their niece gently across the back seat and covered her with a blanket. They watched as Paige pulled her knees to her chest, curled into a fetal position, and closed her eyes.

24

"Ask that policeman there, he'll know."

"Sir? Pardon me, sir: is this the hospital where we're supposed to come to identify victims?"

"No, I'm sorry ma'am. They've set up a temporary facility up the street. Just follow this road a few blocks and you'll see where it is. Take care."

"Thank you, officer. Bless you."

"There's the sign; pull right in there (pause). Are you ready, Honey? You want me to go ask?"

"No, let's go together. Just give me a minute."

"First let me say that we think we've identified your loved one based on some articles we found nearby. I'm not going to let you see him, but I need to ask you some questions."

"What do you mean?"

"Easy, Honey. What do you want to know?"

"Name... and your relationship to the deceased."

"His name or mine?"

"Both, please."

"Kenneth Lee Owens... he's my brother. I'm Thomas J. Owens."

"His date of birth?"

"July 2, 1945."

"Height, weight..."

"Six foot two; about two hundred; blue eyes; gray hair. Are you gonna need his dental records?"

(Pause)

"We'll see. Now, can you tell me what he was wearing? Clothing... jewelry?"

"Never wore a watch, but he probably has a wedding band on his left hand."

"Yes?"

"I think he was wearing a red-checked shirt. Is that right, Beth?"

"Yes, a red-checked shirt and a jean jacket. Blue jeans and boots."

"Any scars or distinguishing things like tattoos?"

"Well, he broke his left arm when we were kids. It was a compound fracture and never healed just right. Kinda overlapped, if you know what I mean."

"That's all I need. We've found your brother. He's a very strongly built man for his age, isn't he?"

"You're not seeing him at his best."

"I don't want you to worry... we're going to take care of Kenneth. With your permission, we need to keep him here for another day to perform an autopsy. We'll then release him to a funeral home of your choice. There's a counselor in the other room to advise you on the ones we have in town and the alternatives available to you."

"Should we bring in some of his clothes for the funeral home?"

"Like I said, the counselor in the other room will advise you on that. There's one more thing."

"Yes?"

"A significant portion of your brother has not yet been recovered. How would you like for us to proceed if we are able to recover?"

(Sobbing)

"We'll give you our names and where you can contact us in Indiana. We'll come back for him, Honey. We won't leave him behind."

Within hours after the tornado struck, one thousand three hundred people were listed as missing, but as they were eventually accounted for, that number quickly dwindled. Many people were reported as being trapped in their destroyed homes. The day after the storm, seventeen people were pulled alive from the rubble. The Missouri Emergency Management Agency reported almost one thousand people injured. Of the one hundred forty-six sets of remains recovered, one hundred thirty-four were positively identified. Due to the horrific injuries suffered by some victims, different sets of remains were from the same person and further reduced the initial estimate of fatalities. The official death toll from the Joplin tornado was one hundred sixty. The tornado also caused one indirect fatality when a policeman was struck by lightning while assisting with recovery efforts the day after the storm.

25

When a raindrop falls and strikes the bare surface of the earth, the soil explodes into tiny particles. These small, almost microscopic fragments - suspended in the accumulating runoff from a rainstorm - percolate into openings in the soil until the earth is saturated and water - in response to gravity - begins to flow downhill. Water can accumulate in depressions, forming temporary pools or permanent ponds and lakes. Most often – like a living thing, which it is, of course – water takes the path of least resistance through the Earth's topography, flowing across the surface of the land, gathering volume and velocity as small creeks feed rivers of modest size like the Flatrock, Blue, and Driftwood Rivers in south-central Indiana. These tributaries in turn converge to form even larger rivers downstream like the White, which pours its poorly named, sediment-laden waters into the Wabash, which joins the Ohio near the pocket city of Evansville at what is known as a *confluence*. Ultimately, over geologic time, a solitary drop of rain that once fell on the fields in Bartholomew County, Indiana - and the sediment that it transported – might have helped to grow the delta at the mouth of the Mississippi upon which sits the City of New Orleans. Such is the interconnectivity of Nature that a *single* thing can have a long term, cumulative impact.

A watershed is an expanse of land where this surface water converges to a *single* point, and the flow joins another water body, such as a river. Each watershed is separated topographically from adjacent watersheds by some sort of geographical barrier such as a ridge, hill, or mountain. In other words, a watershed is like a funnel that collects water within a defined geographic area and channels it to a single point... most often for a purpose. Nature's purpose might be to create a delta that moderates tidal fluctuations, protects the shoreline of a continent from wave erosion, and provides estuarine habitat for aquatic organisms as well as migratory waterfowl. Man has used the discharge points of watersheds to: build mills to grind grain or saw timber, collect and store water for agricultural and domestic use, ameliorate flooding during times of plenty; augment flow for barge traffic in times of want, and especially to generate electrical power.

There is inevitability to the flow of water: You might delay it; you might alter its course; but over time, it will go where Nature determines it must. Hydrologists can provide any number of analytical equations to prove that the volume of water discharged at the end of a watershed can be calculated by adding up the volume of flow from its tributaries. But in truth, a watershed accumulates life and discharges a greater being at its confluence.

The Owens family kept themselves busy. Their private mourning was linked by an unspoken connectivity that framed everyone's dull labor, an understanding - or at least the hope - that time would pass more quickly through work. But what was once a forward motion toward a new life now seemed to have been checked. For Tom and Elizabeth - who with Kenny had carefully planned the move eastward in the preceding months - the past receded behind them as the future appeared to move further away. It seemed that the family's fate was balanced on a knife edge of emotion.

Elizabeth, the twins, and Scout helped at the hospital where Paige had been admitted for observation, volunteering for whatever chores the professional staff asked them to do until Paige was released. Elizabeth did not allow herself the time to grieve for her brother-in-law; there were the children to look after. *Later,* she told herself: *When we get settled, there'll be time enough.*

Paige appeared to have insulated herself inside an emotional cocoon, but in fact, she was very much aware of her surroundings. *I'll manage my own recovery,* she thought, *and on my own time frame. No one's going to tell me how I'm supposed to feel or when I'm supposed to get better.* Unconsciously, almost instinctively, her thoughts began to bend toward filling the void left in her life by her father's passing, and in those times, she thought of Matt, and mentally scolded herself for her selfishness. This would have come as a surprise to members of her family who thought from her remoteness that she had been permanently damaged and might never recover.

Tom, Don, and Matt at first joined the search and recovery teams but eventually transitioned to help with the debris removal once the professional responders came onto the scene. Their construction mentality and experience with heavy equipment proved useful in the days following the tornado, and their work proved therapeutic. Each man labored for his own reasons: Don through a sense of service, Matt in anger, and Tom for redemption.

In the few days that the family remained in Joplin, they camped out at the hospital parking lot in their undamaged trucks and trailers. Restrooms and showers had been set up by the American Red Cross, and meals were provided by the Salvation Army and other church groups. On the day the coroner released Uncle Kenny's remains for cremation, the Owens began to make their plans to leave. Early the next morning - as the family's two vehicles sat idling in the mortuary parking lot – Tom and Elizabeth took possession of the small cherry wood box containing Kenny's remains and left Joplin, Missouri behind them. Just before midnight, the caravan arrived at the family homestead on a low ridge west of the Flatrock River bottoms. The trailers' wheels were chocked, the hitches released from the trucks, and the family set up its semi-permanent camp by starlight.

On the Saturday after Memorial Day weekend, a service was held for Kenneth Lee Owens at the Old Union United Church just north of Owens Bend of the Flatrock River. The little church – established in 1815 – seemed proportional to the small number of mourners who showed up to pay their respects. The congregation was comprised primarily of the extended Owens family and their friends.

Tom started off the proceedings, knowing that if he had to speak for any length of time, he would not be able to get through the day, so he left that to others.

"It seems that the only time this family gets together is for weddings and funerals," he said with a half-smile. "Thank you all for coming today. After this memorial, we'll have a short service at graveside. On behalf of Kenny's daughter, Paige, please join us back here for refreshments in the assembly room downstairs."

The preacher then read a few obligatory lines from the Bible that seemed - to him - appropriate for a man he had never met.

"Kenneth Owens, like his brother Tom, was in the construction business," he intoned. "God speaks to us through his disciples in times of hardship; John, chapter fourteen, verses one to three:"

Do not let your hearts be troubled. Trust in God; trust also in me. In my Father's house are many mansions; if it were not so I would have told you. I am going there to prepare a place for you. And if I go and prepare a place for you, I will come back and take you to be with me that you also may be where I am.

"Kenneth built homes... but these are just temporal, material conveniences of the flesh. Second Corinthians Chapter five, verses one through five:"

Now we know that if the earthly tent that we live in is destroyed, we have a building from God, an eternal house in heaven not built by human hands. Meanwhile we groan, longing to be clothed with our heavenly dwelling, because when we are clothed, we will not be found naked. For while we are in this tent, we groan and are burdened, because we do not wish to be unclothed but to be clothed with our heavenly dwelling, so that what is mortal may be swallowed up by life. Now it is God who has made us for this very purpose and has given us the Spirit as a deposit, guaranteeing what is to come.

Matt squirmed in the pew next to Paige as he heard the words the preacher was speaking about the man that Matt revered as a father. From before he could remember, Kenny had always been in his life, and he heard the minister's words, words that he did not think conveyed enough of a portrayal of Kenny's life and point of view. Matt alternated between wanting to speak his piece and remaining silent, afraid that what he had to say would be offensive to the Owens family – not the California branch that he had known all his life – but the locals from all over Indiana. He and Paige had discussed his feelings the night before, and he turned to her now for assurance. She squeezed his forearm. After the preacher had finished, Matt rose and walked to the front of the church – pausing briefly to place a hand atop the box containing Kenny's ashes – before proceeding to the pulpit. He began:

"This is not the way it was supposed to be. This is not the way it's going to end. Kenny Owens was like a lot of folks in this country; he worked all his life to achieve the American Dream, that if you worked hard enough, you could achieve anything. And for a while, it seemed like he did just that.

"He and his brother Tom moved to California after the war," he continued. "Right off the farm here in Indiana. These two brothers went because they shared a vision of prosperity that extended beyond this land bounded by the Blue and the Flatrock Rivers. They went because it meant opportunity for their families yet to be born. They went because they had confidence in themselves and in the future.

"Today, Kenny has come home. He's come back with his daughter Paige, with his brother Tom and his wife Elizabeth and their children. He's come back to be with his wife, Judith."

Matt paused, took a deep breath, and continued.

"Some of you might be thinking that he returned to the place of his birth because he had no choice, that his great dream played out somewhere in California and now he returns - that we all have returned - broken by a system, by a way of life that is in of itself, broken… and that the great dream is just a dream and not a reality. Well, I'm here to tell you that you're wrong.

"Tom and Elizabeth… and Kenny… have come back to their roots because of a sense of optimism and hope. Kenny has not returned home a defeated man; he is *not* a defeated man! And his dream of a better life for his family has not been diminished by his passing.

"It is ironic – considering all that life threw at him - that Kenny lost his life in an accident of nature. Millions of people in America have lost their jobs, their homes and have been displaced like the Owens by this – as the politicians like to say – this 'economic downturn.' More of them lose hope every day."

"Let's remember that this family is not the only one to have suffered from the recent tornado in Joplin. But it's not what happens to you; it's what you do afterwards that makes the difference."

His last words trailing off, Matt stared at the wooden container at the front of the sanctuary and fought back his tears. The vessel seemed far too small. After a few moments, Paige stepped forward to the pulpit. She touched Matt gently on his arm. By her smile she indicated that he should stand by her while reading a poem of her own creation. Matt stepped back as Paige steadied herself by placing both hands on the podium. She looked above the heads of the congregation to the back of the chapel where the rose window of stained glass glowed in the afternoon sun.

Paige spoke with a voice that had been strengthened by sorrow. She had constructed the stanzas of the sonnet and repeated the couplets in her mind during her road-weary recovery across Missouri and Illinois to Indiana. The epitaph became her mantra. The work would never be shared beyond this memorial service. In fact, she considered the poem as punctuation - as an endpoint to a horrible experience that she planned never to speak of again:

"A love held closely does not comprehend.
Until you left, I did not know your grace.
But since that time, all of my vain attempts
Have failed to draw you back to my embrace.
In weightless drift, you sifted through my hands
To fly before me, always out of sight,
I fell to earth to search in shrouded lands.
What was your day became my endless night.
In spirit - though without you incomplete -
I see the world within myself and know.
That it lacks definition, for the sweet
Memory of your face I still hold close - for though
Remembrance frames all that my windowed eyes
Let pass through them - it is my heart that cries."

At the Flatrock Cemetery just north of the Columbus Airport, small American flags attached to wooden dowels were still in place above the servicemen's graves. They had been placed there the previous week by the local Chapter of the Veterans of Foreign Wars. The cheap, printed cotton whipped in the cool, spring breeze and was already fraying on most of the standards. A grave had been opened in the northwest corner of this stone garden. The depth of the excavation was prescribed by law so that when the concrete vault containing a coffin was sealed, the lid of the tomb would be exactly three feet beneath the surface of the soil. Thus, the understanding that upon death, we all have the option to be placed "six feet under" is a misnomer. Even at the end of our lives, we sometimes get less than what we expect.

During the excavation of Uncle Kenny's final resting place, the concrete vault that was installed twenty years earlier to eventually receive his coffin had been exposed along with a portion of Judith's crypt. Seeing this for the first time, Paige shivered and wrapped her arms around Matt's elbow. When the preacher gently suggested that the family leave before the actual internment and closing of the grave, Paige and Matt remained until the vessel containing Kenny's ashes was lowered into the spacious vault and the lid sealed.

The wind winnowed and gentled the sound of slamming doors and starting engines of the cars parked along the River Road. The mourners drove across the Flatrock River bridge, heading back to the reception at the Old Union church, leaving Kenny with his wife, daughter, and Matt under the bending willows, in the soft afternoon sun.

26

The women began to arrive in pickup trucks and older cars at the Owens farm before dawn. Many rode together - their pots, pans and favorite cooking utensils packed into brown paper grocery sacks, placed between them and their still-drowsy children or rattling on the floorboards of the cars. Each bag had the name of its owner written on it with the contents specified. In the trunk of each car was an archive of similar bags, but these contained glassware, coffee cups, plates, and table service -enough for each member of the family that would be in attendance, plus two or more sets for the unexpected, but anticipated worker-guests. No one had prompted the women to include the extra place settings; it was just an inherent practice that they had learned from their mothers.

The men arrived about the same time as their wives, mostly in pickup trucks. Sitting behind them in the beds of the trucks were the *gophers* – young boys who were old enough to help with the construction instead of assisting with the meals. They would "go fer" anything their fathers, uncles, or brothers needed during the day, whether it be a hammer, nails, or even a glass of water. For some it was their first experience at communal construction, and their eyes were wide with both curiosity and dread as they bounced upon the cold, corrugated metal floor of the truck beds, guarding the shifting toolboxes – holding them in place with their skinny legs and over-sized feet.

To all outward appearances, the gathering of people on this early July morning had the look of an old-time barn raising. In fact, there was a similarity, but the work this day had been planned months in advance. Even as the Owens caravan was in transit from California, their relatives in Indiana had met to explore ways to help the new arrivals get settled in. Uncle Kenny's death heightened that imperative.

At his funeral, Tom and his cousins had decided that the Fourth of July weekend was perhaps the perfect time to re-stage the old family reunion at the home place and get a little work done as well. It had taken a month to assemble all the materials, make plans, and determine an order of work. Tasks were divided based on level of skill and expertise and, in some cases, the sheer numbers that might be required for a job. The elders of the extended family viewed the weekend as an opportunity, not only to help Tom's branch of the tree, but also to introduce the younger members of the clan to each other, create new bonds, and re-establish their roots in the soil of their ancestors.

Prior to this scheduled weekend, the male relatives of several branches of the Owens family completed the remodeling of the inside of the home. This included installation of the plumbing for the kitchen and bathrooms, running electrical conduit for power outlets, framing up new walls, and putting in new windows and doors. The ancient oak floors were relieved of their linoleum, sanded, and refinished. One relative who owned an excavation company laid out the drainage system and installed the septic tank. No one considered getting a building permit.

A casual observer might note the archaic separation of the genders and find it quaint. The women and younger female members of the clan appeared to be confined to the preparation, serving and clean-up of the three meals that would be served that day while the menfolk seemed to bear the responsibility of all construction activities. But in practice, no one was discouraged from participating on either side of that operational divide: the idea was to pitch in somewhere and have a task, or you'd have one assigned to you quickly.

In an area beside the house where it was anticipated that the midday sun would throw a comforting shadow, one of the older men began to crank an auger in the soft ground to excavate a post hole.

"You two," he called to Scout and another boy who stood nearby watching with their hands in their pockets. "Run over to those planks and bring about three of them back here."

The two boys responded quickly. Running to opposite ends of a stack of rough-sawn poplar one-by-twelve boards, where - despite wanting to demonstrate their strength to each other – they discovered that they could lift only one of the ten-foot boards at a time. Awkwardly at first, they turned the board vertically and cupping their right hands underneath the splintered edge, stumbled with the weight to where the man was digging the hole.

"Now," the man said a little more gently. "Lay that board beside this hole so that the end is at the hole and point the other end out there." He indicated the general direction with his hand, and the boys complied. "Now, go get two more and lay them end-to-end; that way I'll know where to dig the next hole."

The boys rushed back to the stack of wood. By the time they returned with the second board, the man had completed the first hole and was starting on the second.

"Good job," the man said. "Now I'm going to need nine more boards; three more boards placed beside the ones that are on the ground; four-wide. You understand?"

"Mister," Scout asked. "What are you building?"

"*We're* building a table to eat on!" Jim Ogilvie answered. "Your daddy's building the t-braces over there. As soon as we get the posts in the ground, you can help me nail these planks on top. Once the table is up, we'll roll those rounds of firewood that ain't been split over here, stand 'em up, and build some benches to sit on. What do you think about that?"

Now understanding the importance of their jobs, the boys raced back to the stack of planks and began to solemnly lay them in place on the grass. Jim leaned on his posthole digger, and laughing to himself, wiped the sweat off his brow and went back to his digging.

Inside the house, the women began to assemble the first of the three meals, a hearty breakfast that would be served after the men had gotten organized and allocated the building tasks among themselves. Coffee was perking in two large thirty-cup carafes on the soapstone counter along the wall. A little girl – scolded not to touch the hot, gleaming silver pots – delicately lined up a multitude of mismatched cups retrieved from the brown grocery bags while a boy of about the same age meticulously folded the paper sacks and stacked them in the corner, to be retrieved later when all the meals had been served and the dishes were done.

Paige stood by the gas stove, mincing clumps of pork sausage into smaller pieces with a wooden spatula as the meat simmered in an over-sized iron skillet. She kept stirring and turning the meat until it had cooked down to smaller brown particles and appeared ready for the next step.

"Aunt Elizabeth," she called. "I think it's done."

Elizabeth joined her niece at the stove and inspected the contents of the pan.

"Turn the heat down, now," she said. "That's some lean sausage; we don't need to drain off the grease. Keep moving it around while I fetch the milk."

Paige kept up her stirring as Elizabeth began to slowly pour the white liquid into the pan. Small, brown globules of grease were rising to the surface of the mixture.

"This is the secret to really good gravy," Elizabeth said. "Some people use water, but there is no substitute for whole milk. Now, when it starts to bubble, we'll add the sifted flour… about a cup or two."

After the flour was added, Paige continued to stir until the gravy began to thicken. Then she added seasoned pepper. Elizabeth, inspecting the progress of biscuits in the oven below, took a spoon from her apron and dipped it into the gravy. She blew gently across the spoon before tasting.

"That's just perfect, honey. They'll make a couple of farm girls out of us yet! Now let's take that off the burner and put it in the crock pot to stay warm. Don't want it too thick; it'll cook down a little."

Using potholders against the heat, the two women lifted the heavy iron skillet from the stove and poured the heavy, sage-scented gravy into an awaiting electric slow cooker on the counter.

"That's one!" Elizabeth laughed as she took a sheet of browned biscuits out of the oven. "Start another, honey; we're going to need at least three more batches."

The work in the first few hours after dawn amounted to organizing materials and apportioning labor. In the kitchen, Elizabeth and Tom's sister, Sandy, divided up the chores between the older women, the girls, and the young children. Those that could cook were assigned to prepare specific meal items – like Paige, who made the gravy and Elizabeth who baked the biscuits. Younger children of grade school age were shepherded by the teenagers in place-setting the rough-hewn tables, serving the workers, replenishing the food, cleaning up after each meal, and helping prepare for the next. It was understood that the kitchen crew would serve themselves only after the men had eaten and gone back to work. Their subservience was not intended to be a demeaning condition, merely an efficient expedient.

Outside the kitchen, the men had divided up into three crews: Matt, Don, and three of his cousins of similar age were responsible for roofing the house. Their time before breakfast was spent unloading the plywood sheeting and bundles of asphalt shingles from the Lowes flatbed truck, strategically positioning the materials at points around the house where they would be out of the way yet easily accessed when work commenced after breakfast.

Teenage boys - too old to be gophers and too young and unskilled for construction - were assigned to the painting crew; their morning was spent scraping the old paint from the clapboards of the house, their older supervisor identifying with a chalk mark where rotten wood needed replacement by the carpenter crew.

The remaining men – most of them cousins from Tom's generation - surveyed the old barn, first determining the structural integrity of the stone foundation and the wooden sills that lay upon them, forming the base of the timber-pegged frame of hand-hewn beams. Inspections had determined that the roof needed to be replaced but that the inside skeleton of the building was sound. The men began to pull off the rusted galvanized roofing and weather-worn, gray-grained old siding in preparation for replacing it with the new poplar board and batten.

By the time Elizabeth called everyone to breakfast, most of the siding had been removed from the barn. Matt and his crew had detached the gutters and downspouts from the house, and the painting crew was speckled with hundreds of tiny pieces of ancient paint, curved, and prickly. These boys were subjected to much good-natured joking at the horse trough where all the men washed up. Before sitting down to eat at the recently constructed table and benches, the entire family joined hands as Tom began to recite the Lord's Prayer.

"They's just a bunch of gypsies, I reckon," said the man who owned the feed store down the road, looking toward the Flatrock River – about a mile away to the east - where a thin, diffuse smoke could be seen drifting out through the trees. "I reckon they'll move on of their own accord."

"No sense disturbing a nest of ground bees," said another.

After breakfast, five men raised the barn's new ridgepole into position. Two men scrambled up the gable posts and secured it in place with wooden pegs. Scooting across the thus-secured horizontal beam on their butts, the same two workers positioned the new rafter poles that were lifted to them. They bored peg holes with hand braces, their awls passing through the rafter ends and into the ridgepole. After these angled struts were secured in place, another crew of men placed perpendicular stringers across the rafter poles. Others on the ground slid sheets of galvanized metal roofing up over the sills of the loft to be overlapped and nailed into place, providing shade for another crew planking down the floor of the loft.

Starting before dawn – this assemblage of thirty men, their wives and daughters providing the meals, and the younger boys gophering materials and water – the entire barn was completed in time for supper. Shortly after everyone had sat down to dinner, Don and Matt selected a few pieces of fried chicken and headed to the river and the column of smoke.

27

According to historians, the practice of war-time military bonuses began in 1776 as payment for the difference between what a soldier earned while on duty and what he could have earned had he not enlisted. But after America's Revolutionary war, most of the Continental Army was discharged without this pay in 1781. In 1783, a few hundred war veterans from Pennsylvania marched on the capital of the United States, then in Philadelphia, where Congress was in session; they demanded to be paid their bonuses. When the soldiers surrounded the State House, members of Congress absconded to Princeton, New Jersey, and a few weeks later the Army was called out to drive out their soldier-comrades in arms. In response to that incident, Washington, D.C., the federal district directly governed by the U.S. Congress, was exempt from the restrictions of the *Posse Comitatus Act* which prohibited the use of the U.S. military for domestic police activity.

American soldiers that served in the Spanish–American War did not receive their bonuses either. After World War I, the question of a post-war military service bonus became a political issue when veterans from *The Great War* received only a $60 bonus. In 1919, the American Legion led the political movement for an additional dividend. On May 15, 1924, President Calvin Coolidge vetoed a bill - passed by both houses of Congress - granting bonuses to these men. Known to everyone as *Silent Cal*, the President spoke this time, saying: "Patriotism... bought and paid for is not patriotism." Congress overrode his veto and enacted legislation that entitled each veteran to around eight thousand dollars, but instead of real money, the veterans were issued a *Certificate of Service* that matured in twenty years, not much good for paying rent, utilities, or buying food for your family during hard times.

The Veterans of Foreign Wars pressed the federal government to allow the early redemption of military service certificates, but President Herbert Hoover and Republican congressmen opposed this action, reasoning that the government would have to raise taxes to cover the costs of the payout, threatening the country's recovery from the Great Depression. What happened next should have been predictable - if Hoover had hindsight that stretched back to 1783 – and may also serve as a warning for government-veteran relations in the not-too-distant future.

In January 1932, twenty-five thousand unemployed Pennsylvania veterans marched on Washington, D.C. This so-called *Bonus Army* set up their Hooverville on a swampy, muddy area across the Anacostia River from Washington. Their shelters were constructed of materials scavenged from a nearby dump. Order was maintained by the veterans themselves, who laid out streets, established sanitation facilities, and even held daily parades. To live in the camps, veterans were required to register and prove they had been honorably discharged. On June 17th, with the Bonus Army surrounding the United States Capitol Building, the Senate defeated a Bonus Bill – submitted by the House of Representatives to allow immediate redemption of the Certificates of Service – by a vote of 62-18.

The marchers, displaying an inordinate amount of patience – most had been discharged from service over ten years earlier - waited for President Hoover to act, which he did, but not in the way the veterans expected. On July 28, 1932 the President, through Attorney General William D. Mitchell, ordered the D.C. police to expel the Bonus Army veterans from their ramshackle camp. The police drew their revolvers and shot two former soldiers. One of those killed was William Hushka, an immigrant to the United States from Lithuania, who sold his butcher shop in St. Louis, Missouri and joined the Army when the United States entered the war in 1917. Eric Carlson, of Oakland, California, died that day as well, having survived the terrible trenches of France. Both men are interred in Arlington National Cemetery.

After the shootings, President Hoover ordered the Army to evict the Bonus Marchers from Washington. In an irony that has been lost to history, General Douglas MacArthur led the 12th Infantry Regiment and the 3rd Cavalry Regiment into the battle, supported by six tanks commanded by Major George S. Patton. Thousands of civil servants left their offices that day and lined Pennsylvania Avenue to watch. The Bonus Marchers, believing the troops were marching in their honor, cheered the troops until Patton ordered the cavalry to charge them. The civil servant employees then began yelling, *"Shame! Shame!"*

Following the cavalry charge, the infantry entered the camp with fixed bayonets and deployed adamite gas, an arsenic-based agent that induces vomiting. When the veterans, their families, and followers fled across the Anacostia River, President Hoover ordered the assault stopped. But in a move that presaged his actions during the Korean War - and brought about his removal from command by President Harry Truman - MacArthur ignored the President and ordered a new attack.

During the military operation, Major Dwight D. Eisenhower was one of MacArthur's aides. The future thirty-fourth President of the United States believed it wrong for the Army's highest-ranking officer to lead an action against fellow American war veterans, and he advised MacArthur not to take a public role: "I told that dumb son-of-a-bitch not to go down there," he would say later. "I told him that it was no place for the Chief of Staff."

The Bonus Army incident proved disastrous for Hoover. He lost the 1932 election in a landslide to Franklin Delano Roosevelt. For his part, Roosevelt - a former Secretary of the Navy - opposed the veterans' bonus demands but arranged for his wife Eleanor to visit a Bonus Camp in Virginia unaccompanied. One veteran commented: "Hoover sent the army, Roosevelt sent his wife." To help resolve the veterans' unemployment problem, Roosevelt later issued an executive order allowing the enrollment of twenty-five thousand veterans in the newly formed Civilian Conservation Corps, or CCC. In 1936, Congress authorized the immediate payment of the $2 billion in WW I bonuses. In overriding the President's veto, the House voted 324 to 61 and the Senate vote was 76 to 19.

Roosevelt's granting enlistment into the CCC for the Bonus Army in 1933 resulted in the training of many young men in the United States through the paramilitary discipline provided by elder veterans. After the shameful treatment of the World War I troops at the hands of the government, it might be suggested that, through the CCC, the Bonus men were participants in an extended boot camp for their replacements. Many of the young men of the CCC became the fighting men of World War II. When they came home, these veterans formed no Bonus Army but went back to work rebuilding a nation. Small wonder this group has been called *The Greatest Generation.*

In the interval between 1950 and 1990, returning veterans were not as prized, and one might suggest - *not as feared* - in terms of their numbers or impact on politics. Korean War veterans were considered to have *participated* in a United Nations *action.* Vietnam veterans were shamefully met with protests and vilification from a divided public. For a while, some veteran groups refused these men and women even the solace of joining their military brothers in social organizations. For the first time, terms like *post-traumatic stress disorder* and *Agent Orange* were inserted into the American post-war lexicon. It became common to hear the excuse of *Vietnam Veteran* being used as a justification for homelessness and odd behavior. Cardboard signs declaring destitution because of military service in Southeast Asia seemed to pop up at most busy street intersections in America's larger cities, particularly in the Western United States.

In contrast, veterans of the Iraq Wars were welcomed home – as they should have been - like conquering heroes. This is in direct contrast to the fact that the combat death toll from nearly nine years of war was the lowest of all major American conflicts. But to approach wars in this manner is just a study in statistics.

Every man is a universe, and each human life is precious. One cannot judge victory, defeat, or patriotism based on numbers. A life lost for God and Country in the Civil War – where there were 625,000 fatalities, both Blue and Gray - is as great a loss as one death in Afghanistan. It is how we as Americans treat those who survive our conflicts that does honor to the fallen.

No one could say precisely how the movement started. There were whispered suggestions that a serving officer, unceremoniously relieved from command in Afghanistan, conceived and organized the first wave of what came to be known as the *Watershed Flotilla* in 2010. This man, like many other servicemen and women, had come home to find that there were no jobs and no prospect of employment in a country that was already experiencing a ten-percent unemployment rate among the civilian population. The swelling number of returning veterans just added to the problem. These soldiers also discovered that wounded comrades who had returned before them were not being cared for properly. And like Donovan Owens, many had families that had been dispossessed of their homes through defaulted mortgages and bank repossessions.

When the Watershed Flotilla first came to the attention of the public it aroused fear: Were these veterans going to be organized into armed paramilitary units that would pillage the countryside through which they passed? Was their state-of-mind such that their behavior could not be predicted? And, of course, politicians wondered how such a mass of people might be used for their own partisan purposes.

The movement along the rivers of America was strategically planned. By using this traditional, colonial form of transportation, the group moved in all manner of watercraft from canoes to motorboats or barges – anything that would float, gathering momentum as they travelled downstream. At first the number of participants appeared as a non-threatening trickle, and this was by design. The architect of the crusade – the illusory *General* – had determined that such a pace would appear much less menacing to the local populace allowing the flotilla to accumulate popular support along its routes.

Soldiers are taught to identify the source of hostility and respond with appropriate force until the threat is eliminated. It has been said that when it comes to combat, a soldier fights not for a cause or a political point of view but for the man standing next to him.

There was no announcement, no advertisement in the newspapers, no broadcast over the radio waves or on television, but in the spring of 2011, veterans began to gather at the headwaters of small and large rivers all over America. In parts of the United States where rivers flowed westward, veterans travelled overland to the headwaters and tributaries of the Missouri, the Platte, the Ohio, and the Mississippi. Through invisible, military/scuttlebutt lines of communication, it was understood that all groups should time their movements to arrive in Cincinnati, Ohio by the end of September for an initial encampment. From there, the orders were to proceed upriver to Pittsburgh, Pennsylvania then onto Philadelphia by overland routes before arriving in Washington, D.C. before Veterans Day on November 11, 2011.

Even the initial planning for the gathering of the veterans at Cincinnati had a purpose. Settled in 1788, the city had been named for Lucius Quintus Cincinnatus who was a Roman patrician living in humble circumstances on his own farm until unrest within the empire caused him to be called to serve Rome as dictator. After defeating the enemies of Rome, he gave up his authority and dictatorship and went back to his farm. The immediate resignation of his absolute authority at the end of the crisis has often been cited as an example of service for the greater good, lack of personal ambition, and modesty. In choosing Cincinnati, Ohio as a rendezvous point, the General was hopeful that the city's symbolism would not be lost on politicians in Washington.

This man - known by his shadow-name as *General Clark* – was christened, some suggested, after William Clark, who along with Meriwether Lewis sought the Northwest Passage from 1804-1806 traveling up the watershed of the Missouri River – the newly-purchased Louisiana Territory. The *Louisiana Purchase* and subsequent explorations expanded the territory of the infant United States threefold in less than three years. It was a story the flotilla watermen told at night around riverbank campfires.

To the veterans, the story of Lewis and Clark and the Corps of Discovery – a military expedition – was a further illustration of bureaucratic injustice to soldiers. In 1804 Congress had denied Clark - a Lieutenant in the U.S. Army – the rank, pay, and privileges of Captain for the Expedition despite the insistence of his friend and former subordinate, Captain Meriwether Lewis. However, Lewis kept Clark's inferior rank a secret from his men and treated Clark as his equal in command. Lewis also lobbied for his friend's promotion in rank after the expedition, an example of a soldier fighting for the man standing next to him.

The more historically astute among the veterans suggested a more military-based claim, that their unseen leader had taken his name from William Clark's oldest brother, George Rogers Clark. Known as the *Long Knife* by the Native Indians, G.R. Clark was the *Hero of Vincennes.* By capturing Fort Sackville from the British in 1779, he acquired for the United States the watershed regions now known as Indiana, Kentucky, Ohio, Illinois, Michigan, Wisconsin, and Minnesota - the *Old* Northwest Territory.

It was meaningful to all the members of the Flotilla that the Clarks were brothers and that they were soldiers. But even more important was the fact that G.R. Clark, after funding his expeditions and paying his troops out of his own purse, died in poverty and obscurity, abandoned by the same government he helped to create and protect.

28

The westering sun was still an hour away from setting when Matt and Don began their walk down the dirt road toward the Flatrock, about a mile east of the Owens' farm. For the last few days, on those warm summer evenings when the breeze had not dissipated it from the lower branches of the riverside forest, the young men had seen a lens of smoke hanging above the trees. When the origin of the grayish-blue haze appeared to be extending upstream, indicating an increase in the number of campfires, Don decided the time had come for him to investigate the squatters along the river. Matt had already met with some of them and agreed to come along.

"It's always been said that those that don't learn from history are doomed to repeat it," Matt said as they walked along. "Have you ever heard of the Bonus Army of 1932?"

"No," Don replied.

"Well, you're about to meet the current version. It seems to me like history is cyclic. What I'm trying to understand lately are the roots of our past. I wonder if there isn't some larger force at work that drives men to do certain things over and over without regard for historical memory."

"I knew that you were always interested in history. Sounds like pre-history to me."

"You know, I've been reading this book by Jared Diamond called *Guns, Germs, and Steel*. It's all about how environmental factors influenced the development of civilization from the beginning of time."

"When did you get so intellectual?"

"If you lost your job and were unemployed with everything collapsing around you, you'd start looking for answers too," Matt said. They reached the river and turned north along a levee that had been raised one hundred years earlier by Don's great-grandfather.

"And this guy Diamond has the answers?" Don laughed. "Is he a prophet or something like Nostradamus; does he predict the end of civilization as we know it?"

"No, no, no. He's an evolutionary biologist, a professor of geology at UCLA, actually."

"In hard times, most folks turn to the Bible; what does the Book of Diamond have to say?"

"That's good! That's really good. But seriously, the thing that interests me -and the reason I started reading the book - is I just think there must be some precedent for what's happening in the world today."

The two young men picked up their pace to pass quickly through the spray from a center-pivot irrigator that rotated in a slow but determined progression across the field.

"I knew you liked to study history, and so do I," Don said. "But you're talking pre-history, right?"

"That's an affirmative," Matt said. "I just think there are larger forces at work that determine human actions. I think that this guy has it nailed."

"In five minutes or less," Don said as they approached the point where the grass tractor path crossed the levee. "How so?"

"Take for example how he says we all began as hunter-gatherers, taking what was available in our immediate environment then moving on when the local resources were depleted."

"Okay," Don replied. "I can buy that."

"He then suggests that we became sedentary; that is, we began to put down roots, establish villages and grow crops because the environment changed, available food resources grew limited, and hunter-gatherers were not as successful as those who farmed."

"What do you mean by successful?"

"Well for one thing, did you know that hunter-gatherers only had one offspring every *four* years and that farmers, by comparison - because they had more available food and resources - had on average one offspring *every year*."

"Thank God I'm a country boy!" Don laughed.

"The serious point is that because the sedentary farmers had more offspring, they began to outnumber the hunter-gatherers. And instead of spending all their time trying to find their next meal, they had the time to develop political systems of government, work on crafts, like tools for hunting or weapons, and were basically more organized."

"So what?"

"So what?" Matt replied. "So that explains to me why Europeans, who were basically the more numerous farmers - more organized and technologically advanced - were able to easily overcome indigenous, hunter-gatherer populations in Africa, Asia, and here in North America, the Indians."

"Okay," Don replied. "Again; so, what?"

Matt took a deep breath, stopped walking for a moment just short of the levee.

"The way I got it figured, when we were in California, we were basically hunter-gatherers, taking advantage of the resources that were there. Now those resources have dried up, and we came back here to be farmers. That's the big picture I'm looking at in terms of human behavior."

"Never thought of myself as a Neanderthal," Don laughed.

"Totally different line of ascension. But look at the evidence: you and I are twenty-five years old; Paige is what?"

"Twenty-one."

"Twenty-one," Matt repeated, thoughtfully, adding: "The twins are seventeen and the Scout, he's thirteen. Everyone is four years apart. Hunter-gatherers. I rest my case."

"Wow, that's a reach," Don said. "But I can see how you got there."

"Yeah," Matt replied. "And the cool thing is that over time, there'll end up being more of us than the hunter-gatherers, we'll be more organized and have more offspring; in other words, farmers rule!"

"So, Mister Anthropologist, what about these guys back here along the river?" Don said, gesturing toward the smoky, darkening woods.

"Them?" Matt responded. "I've given that some thought, too. These guys are the herders, shepherds more or less."

"What?"

"I'll explain later. You should know that for the most part, they're all former military, too."

"How do you know that?"

"I came back here recently," Matt said. "Most of them are about your age or a little older. Veterans of the Gulf wars actually; some with tours of Afghanistan like you. I think you'll get along just fine."

Whoa, Don thought. *These guys are going to be tough to move off our land. I wonder if they're armed?*

"I know what you're thinking. How are we going to get these guys off your property? Well, don't worry about that; you'll see that they're herders. They're here just temporarily; they'll move on directly."

"So," Don laughed. "From a cultural standpoint, how do hunter-gatherers, farmers, and herders get along?"

"Jared Diamond says that farmers despise hunter-gatherers as primitive; hunter-gatherers despise farmers as ignorant; and herders despise them both."

"That's just great," Don said, and the two men climbed up the sloped embankment toward the source of the smoke, the setting sun at their backs.

"Attention on deck!" a voice called out as Don and Matt crested the top of the levee and paused for a moment to assess the scene in front of them. In a semi-open area of woods, just below where they stood, a large tarp had been extended over a ridge pole that was lashed between two trees. Bent in the middle with its panels extended like wings by ropes staked into the ground, the canvas formed a roof-like shelter under which about twenty men were standing. Surrounding this central meeting point was an assortment of tents in various types and sizes. The smoke was coming from many small fires located in front of the individual tents that had been established with the intention of warding off mosquitoes rather than providing warmth for the residents. A few folding camp stools and umbrella chairs of different colors circled each campfire. Don was surprised to see two trucks parked at the edge of the woods with a few women sitting on the tailgates. *They must have driven in on the old tractor path to the north*, he thought. A tall man in camouflage fatigues stepped out from under the fly.

"Welcome, gentlemen!" he called. "What can we do for you?"

Don and Matt cautiously descended into the growing darkness of the bottomland woods. Matt waited for Don to say something and hoped that his friend wouldn't sound too confrontational. It appeared that the two of them were outnumbered at least ten to one.

"I guess the question ought to be: what can I do for you?" Don replied. "Y'all are camped out on my family's land." As soon as he spoke, Don realized that the words had come across as a challenge he had not meant to express.

The man in the fatigues approached them without hesitation and, stopping a few feet in front of Don and Matt, snapped to a salute. Instinctively, Don returned the compliment.

"And we're very much in your debt for the temporary quarters you've provided sir," the man replied, dropping his arm and extending his hand to Don. "I'm Major Indiana, Commander of the Indiana Division of the Watershed Flotilla." As Don shook his hand, the major glanced toward Matt with a smile of recognition then turned his attention back to Don. "I understand that you're a brother in arms. Thank you for your service."

Don was stunned. Clearly, Matt had set him up for this encounter, and he struggled as to what his next move should be. Fortunately, the older officer took the lead.

"Why don't you come over to the Briefing Room, son," the major said. "I was just getting ready to go over some logistics with the Company."

Don and Matt followed the major to the tent fly where one soldier was lifting another up to light a Coleman lantern suspended from the ridgepole in the center of the canvas-roof. Most of the men under the awning were dressed in fatigues, and their battledress was of the camouflaged variety – green, tan, or blue variants, depending on the branch of the military in which each man served. The blouse, or shirt, displayed a name but not the person's rank. The major eased through the little crowd and took position in the front of the tent where a four-by-four-foot piece of plywood had been placed on a makeshift easel constructed of sticks lashed together with bailing twine. A map of the

State of Indiana was tacked to the board, and Don noticed that the rivers were highlighted in red. With the canvas fly, tents, campfires, and now the makeshift easel, everything seemed rather Boy Scout-like to Don. He smiled and relaxed.

"Gentlemen, at ease," the major said. "We have a few new people from upriver who have joined us tonight, so I want to give a little orientation before we have a working dinner to discuss the status of our situation. First, I'd like to introduce our host," he added, nodding to the back of the tent where Matt and Don stood. Matt elbowed Don lightly in the ribs.

"Lieutenant Donovan Owens," Don said. "Special Forces, Afghanistan."

"Oo-rah!" a few men exclaimed.

"This land has been in my family since the 1870s," Don continued, then paused and surveyed the faces of the group. "You're welcome here."

"Oo-rah!" came the cry as a few more men joined the chorus, this time much louder.

"And we thank you, brother," the major answered. "Now let's get down to business."

"Is his name really Indiana?" Don whispered to Matt.

"I doubt it. All these guys have fictitious, geographic names. It's meant to help organizationally and provide protection for their families; it's not meant to be deceptive, just a precaution."

"First of all," the major continued, "you newer guys need to get registered. Lieutenant Dan of the Flatrock Company will give you a form to fill out with your name, rank, and serial number for our records. We also need your dates of service and, if you have them on ya, your discharge papers. If you don't have them, you're gonna need to get them to join this group, so before we get too far down river, go get 'em. We also need contact information for next of kin. All this information will be kept at your local post of the American Legion. The Legion has accepted that responsibility and volunteered to provide support services for our group, so this'll give 'em an idea of the numbers they need to feed.

"Along those lines," he continued, "you're guaranteed one hot meal a day, and that'll usually be in the evening, provided by the Ladies Auxiliary. They also bring stuff for breakfast and lunches along with dinner, but you'll have to mess for yourselves along those lines."

"We police ourselves," added the lieutenant. "We operate under a chain of command that's based on your previous rank and date of induction. There are no firearms allowed in camp, so if you brought some with you, take 'em back. Pocketknives, axes, machetes, and brush-clearing tools are okay."

"Cooperation with each other is the key, gentlemen," the major added. "We don't give orders, but we do expect that each of you will do your fair share of work in maintaining order in the camps, and you *will* discipline yourselves. We don't encamp at any place too long to wear out our welcome. We try to stay at established parks and facilities where possible. This is as much for security as it is for visibility and acceptance by the locals. Camping here was a necessity for this Company. But there's another group on the Blue River that's encamped at the City Park in Edinburgh and another at Lowell Bridge on the Driftwood just north of Columbus. All three Companies will rendezvous at Mill Race Park in Columbus the day after tomorrow."

"We leave areas better than we found them," the lieutenant added, gesturing toward a large pile of trash and debris beside one of the pickup trucks. "If you see some piece of junk in the river, along the bank, or at your campsite, throw it in your boat. The Legion will take care of disposing of it for us."

"Finally," the major said, "before we sample some of the fine food the ladies have brought for us this evening, let me say this: you're not on a picnic; you're on a mission. The mission is to build awareness of our needs – what we are entitled to as returning veterans. You represent those who can't be here with us because they are incapacitated or in hospitals. You stand and fight for your brothers and sisters who made the ultimate sacrifice - to ensure that their families get the support they need and deserve. And you will not forget those who, by their own hand, gave up their lives as well." The Major paused to let his last statement sink into the minds of his listeners.

“We are doing this to win hearts and minds, people,” he concluded. “Hearts and minds that will rally to our cause and build a collective, political momentum as we travel across this great country on our way to Washington. Any questions?”

There was silence as the major looked each man in the eye and received a short, terse nod in response.

“Okay,” he said with a smile. “Chow time!”

29

It was after midnight when Don and Matt left the river encampment and started walking back to the farm in the dark. They had joined the group for dinner under the tarp and learned something of the organization and timetable of the movement.

Except for the Major, it turned out that the rank of the officers was largely ceremonial and assigned or voted on by each group. General Clark had structured a chain of command down to the level of his immediate subordinates, but beyond that, the participants organized themselves. His four *colonels* were assigned to address security issues with local law enforcement, handle publicity, provide national political interface, and coordinate the assistance of support groups like the American Legion. A *Major* was assigned – and took the name – of each state. A major's role was to keep the different groups within a state moving, either by land or by water, and to settle any issues when the groups encountered each other at the confluences of watersheds.

Each river had its captain who commanded a Company named for the tributary, such as the Flatrock Company with which Don and Matt had just spent the evening. Depending on the number of soldiers in each company, the men were organized into smaller groups or *messes* for the purpose of meals and for the policing of each encampment. By far the largest of the Indiana companies was the Wabash Company, followed by the White River (East Fork) and White River (West Fork). By comparison, the Flatrock Company was relatively small.

"It will be interesting to see what happens when these different groups come together for the first time," Matt said. "We should head down to Columbus in the next day or two to check it out; there might be some conflict."

"You might be surprised," Don replied. "I have a feeling that there'll be a lot less disagreement among the troops than you might think. These soldiers will position themselves based on their rank and dates of service, with the older veterans stepping forward to resolve disputes. It's a military mindset that doesn't have a civilian equivalent."

"I don't know. Some of those guys seemed a little sketchy to me."

"No doubt. But you know, when you come back in-country, even on leave, you miss the familiarity of command structure, the brotherhood that builds in a combat situation, and the security of knowing that your buddy has your back. It's the absence of these absolutes that creates a problem for these guys in civilian life. It's like a cockroach in the middle of a room: it panics until it can find a wall. Being a part of a group like we were with tonight is probably the best therapy for a lot of them."

"I can see that," Matt replied. "When all is said and done, the whole flotilla idea is probably a great transition model for a returning vet." Matt paused for a moment. "I wonder if that's one of the things the organizers had in mind when they conceived this thing."

"You know," Don replied thoughtfully, "I think you might have something there. If this thing can be pulled off without any violence and these guys can gain the support of the public as they move along, the political aspect of their demands will take care of itself."

"Because the public will be behind them long before they get to Washington."

"There's an inevitability to it," Don replied.

"Sure seems like it to me," Matt said. "In the meantime, these guys – a lot of them unemployed and without any kind of plans right now, are assimilated back into the world, partly through the fact that they have a mission and because that duty forces both the Flotilla and the public to support each other. It's goddammed genius!"

"Maybe. We'll have to see how it shakes out down river."

"Have you given any thought to joining them?"

"Not a chance. I've done my service. I know my dad would say we need to focus on the family right now. You'd probably like to be a leader in this group, wouldn't you? Probably appeals to your sense of justice, huh?"

"Well, they wouldn't take me anyway. I have no service record."

"You don't know how lucky you are to have a heart murmur."

"I don't know," Matt said wistfully. "I feel like I missed something."

"You're my best friend and brother," Don said. "Believe me, you haven't missed anything."

The two young men saw the mercury vapor light from the farm in the distance, and each felt a wave of emotional and physical exhaustion wash over them.

"Damn," Don said. "For the middle of the summer, it sure gets a little chilly in the bottoms, huh?"

"I am so ready to hit the hay," Matt responded. "And not just figuratively speaking."

"Yeah, sleeping in the barn loft is pretty nice," Don laughed. "Except that for a while there, the outhouse was a hundred feet too close."

"Maybe so," Matt replied. "Thank God we got the septic system in; otherwise, it would have been a hundred feet too far away this winter!"

The two friends had settled into their barn loft cots. The electric lantern had been dimmed down. The rest of the family was asleep inside the partially remodeled farmhouse; Tom and Elizabeth in the master bedroom, Paige in her own room, Julie and Jenny, appropriately enough, on twin beds in a third bedroom, and Scout on the pullout couch in what would eventually be the living room.

"Are you asleep?" Matt asked.

"Not just yet," Don answered. "I'm too tired."

"Do you mind if we talk for a while?"

"What's on your mind?"

"I've got a job," Matt said. "I start next week."

"No kidding?" Don said. "Doing what?"

"It seems like they're building a new interstate between Indianapolis and Evansville," Matt replied. "You know the Major? He was a civil engineer on that project before he got called up by the National Guard. He gave me a contact at the Indiana Department of Transportation. Had an interview and bingo! They're giving me a state truck, too."

"Well, I'll be damned!" Don said. "You *do* know something about construction management."

"I'll be working out of the Seymour office down the road; I would have operated a backhoe if I had to, whatever it took. But it seems like they need some people that know how to deal with contractors..."

"And considering that's what you are…"

"Exactly!"

"That's really good news," Don said sitting up on the side of his cot. "Do my folks know?"

"Yep. I told them as soon as I knew that I had the job. They're happy for me, although I think they'll miss the extra hands around the place."

"Aw, everything is pretty much done on the house except for maybe a little drywall and paint. They'll just miss your smiling face."

"Maybe, but now I feel like I have something more to contribute than just a strong back."

"C'mon. With all that's happened in the last five years since I've been gone, you've got to know that you're as much a part of this family as I've ever been. Don't you see that?"

"I sure would like for it to be like that," Matt replied. "I think the world of your folks and of course, your Uncle Kenny was like a father to me."

"And what about Paige?"

"What about Paige?"

Don laughed. "Man, everyone in the family knows you both have a thing for each other. It was obvious to me before we left California. It just took some time for you to figure it out. Do you really intend to leave her behind?" Don paused for a few moments while he gathered his thoughts. "Wait a minute! You're not thinking about taking Paige with you, are you?"

"No, no, no!" Matt laughed. "That's not the problem. We're in love, and we're putting our roots down here. With the insurance money from her dad, Paige is pretty much set. Hell, Social Security will help her finish her education as well. She wants to go to I.U. And now with this new job, I have something to offer her. We're getting married."

"What?"

"We've already made plans," Matt said. "I'm going to ask your dad tomorrow, as a stand-in for Kenny, of course. I thought you should know."

"I can't say that I'm surprised. You're a good man, Matt. She could do a lot worse."

"Maybe, but until very recently, I've been feeling aimless and unworthy. It wasn't all about the money; but to some extent, I guess it's my pride as well."

"Are you nervous about asking the old man?"

"A little," Matt said. "Actually, I'm really nervous."

"Well, don't be," Don laughed. "I'll plow the row; I'll give my dad a heads-up, but I think that he and mom have suspicions already."

"So how about being my best man? We're planning for October."

"I'll make sure I'm around for that, buddy."

"Are you planning on going somewhere anytime soon?"

"It's all your fault," Don replied. "All the way here you got me thinking. There are people in this country that are really hurting, decent folks camped out at Walmarts like a bunch of migrants and others afraid of them because they see what their future might be as well. I've seen workers inside Walmart struggling for a decent wage to raise their families, packs of men on the move with no foreseeable future, like those guys that jumped us outside of Elk City. Now tonight, groups of veterans not getting what's coming to them."

"I heard that there's now a bunch of New York City people camped out in a park near Wall Street. They claim to represent the ninety-nine percent of the population that has been screwed by a government that supports the banks at the expense of the working man," Matt added.

"I heard that, too," Don said. "These things are not what I was fighting for overseas."

"So, what do you plan to do?"

"I've talked to my dad about it. He says I can borrow Uncle Kenny's truck if I return it. I plan to drive around and see what's going on, for a while at least. Get some answers."

"How long do you plan on being gone?" Matt asked.

"Only for the length of time it takes to get back a little self-reliance and economic independence. There's a girl in Flagstaff I want to go check on. My plan is to bring Uncle Kenny's truck back along with the girl."

"Why, you son of a gun," Matt cried. "How long has this been going on? When were you going to let me know?"

"We've been talking on the phone nearly every day since the family left Arizona," Don laughed. "I've even taken to writing letters occasionally; I've been told that I'm very persuasive."

"Well, I'll be damned! I doubt that there's anything in this world that can surprise me anymore."

A week after leaving the farm in Indiana, Don was preparing to depart Flagstaff for the return home. As he finished loading Heather's belongings into the back of the truck, he helped her up into the cab. When he got in on the driver's side, she slid across the bench seat against him and kissed him.

"I don't start my new job at I.U. until the end of August," Heather added. "That should give us plenty of time to get to know each other a lot better! We're really doing this aren't we?"

"Yep," Don said. "Which direction you want to go first?"

"Can we stop at the Diner before we head out? I'd like to say goodbye to Rosey and Bob."

"Sure. We're in no hurry. I figure that we should take a circuitous route to get back to the farm, maybe head up into the mountains of Montana and drive down the Yellowstone River to where it joins the Missouri. After that, we just follow the river back to St. Louis."

"That sounds awesome!" she giggled. "But let's get some coffee first!"

30

Autumn in the Midwest is a sensual experience; there's a definite smell in the air and a granular taste on the tongue. Sunlight filters and refracts through a golden haze of crop dust rattled from fields of sun-dried corn and beans, their residual stems and stalks flailed and pulverized into fine particles by the combine. The heavier plant material settles to the soil surface, forming a protective mulch against the approach of fall rains and the scour of winter wind and snow. One can feel and taste the lighter particles that are suspended in the cool air, absorbing the tongue's moisture as they are inhaled. Dust angels sift through forest trees and window screens, dancing down the low angle of the sun's rays. Sounds are winnowed and softened. In small creeks and rivers like the Flatrock, the normal crash of tumbling water is muted with the reduced flow as the river slides, tannin-stained along a carpet of newly fallen leaves.

In the last week of September, the neighbors and relatives that helped put the Owens' farmhouse and barn back to rights were engaged in a less arduous, but important task, building a wedding place for Paige and Matt in the woods near the river. The couple had chosen the northern area of the woods where the Flatrock Company of the Flotilla had encamped. The ground was open in between the trees and relatively free of weeds since the veterans had cleared most of the undergrowth when they had set up their tents.

A wedding arbor was erected beneath two large, twin sycamores that appeared to grow out of a central root system, forming a perfect *V*. Paige and Matt had discovered this object of natural symbiosis while on a walk in the woods, and the bride-to-be immediately recognized the implied matrimonial metaphor.

A large dance floor – fifty feet by fifty feet - was constructed by digging holes and setting treated posts in an eight-foot square pattern around a central maple tree. Joists were then strung between the posts to form the floor's framework. The posts at the perimeter were left at full length to support an outer railing, but the inner posts were cut off with a chainsaw, after which the men nailed down one by six-inch planks of raw oak flooring. When they finished, the entire dance floor was suspended a foot off the ground with only one step up required for access. A strapping of horizontal planks was nailed against the outside posts – forming a safety barrier – and benches were constructed around the interior perimeter of the dance floor, including curved seats artfully fashioned to encircle the central maple tree.

There was no rehearsal the night before the wedding. Instead, the Owens women and older children set up picnic tables and chairs beneath the trees surrounding the dance floor. The men extended wires from side posts to the central tree on which they hung clear incandescent light bulbs. The branches of the maple tree were wrapped with coils of small, twinkling Christmas lights. A generator was positioned at a distance in the woods and shielded by hay bales to reduce the sound of its exhaust. As darkness began to fall, a switch was thrown, and the entire area was illuminated like a carousel. A band of old-timers who volunteered to play music for the wedding reception tested the autumnal acoustics by striking up a waltz.

On her wedding day, Paige climbed into a rented horse-drawn carriage at the farmhouse with her Aunt Elizabeth and the twins, Jenny and Julie, who were her maids of honor. They proceeded north along the county road, turning east toward the river an hour before sunset. Tom met the gig at the edge of the woods and helped first the twins, then his wife, and finally his niece, Paige, down from the carriage. As the girls and Elizabeth proceeded down the lantern-lined path into the woods to join Don and Scout at the twin sycamores, Tom paused for a moment before Paige took his arm. She wore a simple, but elegant, sleeveless V-neck dress of white chiffon that had been her mother's.

"You look absolutely lovely, Paige," Tom said, his eyes beginning to mist with the memory of his brother's wedding to Judith. "I truly wish that your father and mother were here."

Paige took the handkerchief from her uncle's jacket pocket and dabbed his eyes. Then she kissed him on the cheek and whispered in his ear, "I think they are."

At the wedding arbor that their family and friends had fashioned of entwined grapevines, the two lovers recited their vows. In her bouquet of dried flowers and interwoven orange bittersweet, Paige had secreted two small pieces of paper - each rolled and tied with a ribbon, just in case she or Matt might forget their vows. The scrolls would not be needed today.

Paige began:

"There is an unseen stream that flows to you,
A quiet highway to your heart. In sleep,
Where in my dreams I move, trusting and true,
I give my heart to you for you to keep.
The midday sun emits a pallid shade
As, in my arms, I've held your brighter light.
The diamond fire from dull stars seem to fade
When in my dreams, your memory walks the night.
Like willows at the river's edge, my heart -
A wandering stream that does not know its place -
Receives the bough's caress. When we're apart,
The compass of my soul turns on that grace.
I mark the time 'til I see you again,
And hear your voice upon the fragrant wind."

Matt replied:

"There's a warm wind out tonight, and a full moon is riding high,
The Milky Way and the stars are suspended from the sky,
A tide of memories is bearing me away,
And thoughts of you are candled in my eye.
To that place within your heart, where you hold my memories,
Come take me now, and entwined with you,
in the night beneath the trees,
We'll make love within the woods, bend to gentle winds,

And in each other's arms watch sunsets die.
Why don't we just steal away? Set out on the eventide,
And let one heart be our pilot and the moon path be our guide,
We'll find a secret place to seal our lyric love,
And dance across the mountains of the moon."

The dance was still going in full force when Matt led his bride away to the waiting carriage. They bumped along the old tractor path at the edge of the woods until they were half a mile south of the continuing celebration. Matt took a spare lantern from the driver, climbed out of the carriage, setting the lamp on the ground and lifted Paige out of her wedding coach. Without a word, the driver clucked up the horse, and the gig pulled away into the night, its oil lamps swaying as it rolled toward the farmhouse. Matt picked up his light, took Paige by the hand and led her into an area deep in the woods where a light seemed to be growing under the dark mantle of the forest.

Paige was both excited and overwhelmed as Matt led her to an opening among the trees where an antique brass bed was illuminated by dozens of candle-lit lanterns hanging from the branches of trees. Suspended from an overhead limb was a filmy canopy of mosquito netting that tented the wedding bed.

The glow from the candles burnished the metal of the bedframe, and a slight wind rustled the trees, causing golden leaves to float down around them. As Matt lifted the protective mesh, Paige turned her back to him, staring into the darkness as he unzipped her gown and let it fall to the ground. She stepped out of the dress and sat down on the bed behind him, wrapping her arms around his shoulders. Then she moved, pulling herself against his back. She kissed his ear and laid her chin on his left shoulder. They both gazed into the darkness toward the distant sounds coming from upriver.

Matt gently pulled Paige's arms from around his chest and turned to face her. She looked directly into his face, tears forming at the corners of her eyes. Without blinking, she began to cry. Matt pushed the hair away from her forehead with his fingertips and smoothed a teardrop on her cheek with the thumb of his right hand. Her lower lip quivered as they kissed, and they held each other tightly without speaking.

In the secret darkness of the riverside, with only the murmuring river as witness, the guttering candles provided the only light by which the two young people silently and urgently made love. Afterwards when the lanterns had burned out, they lay together on the old bed, holding onto each other, huddled under the milky gauze of mosquito netting. Paige lay against her husband with her head on his chest, her warm tears diffused by the sweat of his body.

Sometimes in life – and not by accident – God grants us a splendid grace, a continuity of personality between generations linked by blood. On the eighteenth of July in the following year, Paige gave birth to a little dark-haired boy that - everyone remarked - looked like his grandpa from the very day he drew breath. He was twenty-one and a quarter inch long and weighed seven pounds, four ounces. They named him Owen Kenneth Forrest, but his Uncle Donnie always called him Okie, for short.

Michael V. Harding is an environmental scientist and one of the leading technical experts in the field of erosion and sediment control. A graduate from Purdue University, Michael has over forty years of experience in resource management, mined land reclamation, wildlife habitat development, and nonpoint source pollution control both in the United States and overseas. Michael specializes in the evaluation, research, development, and application of cost-effective erosion control materials and techniques. He is a Certified Professional Erosion and Sediment Control Specialist (CPESC), Certified Erosion, Sediment, and Stormwater Inspector (CESSWI), and a Trainer of Record for California's QSP/QSD program. Throughout his career, he has provided legal support and expert witness for domestic and international mediation, arbitration, and litigation cases involving soil erosion, re-vegetation, and reclamation.

Michael is a three-time past president of the International Erosion Control Association (IECA) and Chief of Council for the IECA's International Regional Council. He is one of the leading technical authors on subjects related to erosion and sediment control, resource management, and post-fire hazard mitigation. Regularly, he teaches seminars and workshops on the subject of storm water pollution and has written numerous instruction manuals to support his teaching.

He is an adjunct faculty member of San Diego State University's College of Civil and Environmental Engineering. Michael has been the invited speaker at the National Academy of Sciences, the National Transportation Research Board, and was a contributing author to the book *Environmental Restoration, Science and Strategies for Restoring the Earth,* edited by John Berger (Island Press). He was also contributing author to the book *Industrial Applications of Natural Fibres*, edited by Jorg Mussig (John Wiley and Sons, Ltd.).

Michael conceived and led the Flight of Discovery (FOD) from 2004-2006, an aerial environmental expedition along the Lewis and Clark Historic Trail to document 200 years of environmental change during the National Bicentennial of the voyage of the Corps of Discovery.

Made in the USA
Columbia, SC
13 October 2024

43491382R10104